The LEARNING RELATIONSHIP

HOW TO SEE LOVE AS A SYSTEM AND
BUILD ONE THAT CAN GROW

PRINCE-JAMES SMITH, PHD

A research-informed guide to seeing love as a living system, understanding the patterns that shape connection, and building a relationship that can learn, repair, and grow.

THE LEARNING RELATIONSHIP examines what happens when love is understood not only as emotion, chemistry, or commitment, but as a living system shaped by patterns, feedback, behavior, assumptions, repair, and shared growth. Grounded in systems thinking, cognitive psychology, behavioral science, applied behavior analysis, ACT-informed values-based action, and relationship insight, this book offers a practical and psychologically informed framework for individuals and couples seeking to understand what they bring into love, recognize recurring patterns, strengthen personal mastery, challenge mental models, use conflict as information, repair with intention, and build a relationship capable of learning over time.

This book is designed to work alongside **The Learning Relationship Workbook,** which helps readers apply the concepts from these pages to real- world relationship patterns, reflection, repair, and intentional growth.

THE LEARNING RELATIONSHIP

Readers experiencing relationship abuse, coercion, threats, violence, severe emotional distress, thoughts of self-harm, or safety concerns should seek immediate support from qualified professionals, emergency services, or appropriate crisis resources. This book is intended for educational reflection, self-assessment, and personal growth. It is not psychotherapy, diagnosis, medical advice, legal advice, or a substitute for individualized care from qualified professionals.

The concepts presented in this book draw from business principles, cognitive psychology, behavioral science, relationship research, and applied self-reflection. Readers are encouraged to use the material thoughtfully, honestly, and responsibly.

Quantity sales and special discounts are available on quantity purchases by corporations, associations, and others. For details, contact the publisher at the address above.

Orders by U.S. trade bookstores and wholesalers. Email Michael@BeyondPublishing.net

The Beyond Publishing Speakers Bureau can bring authors to your live event. For more information or to book an event contact the Beyond Publishing Speakers Bureau speak@BeyondPublishing.net

The Author can be reached directly at BeyondPublishing.net

Manufactured and printed in the United States of America distributed globally by BeyondPublishing.net

BEYOND PUBLISHING

New York / Los Angeles / London / Sydney / Bangkok

ISBN Hardcover: 979-8-9962262-5-2

ISBN Softcover: 979-8-9962262-2-1

DEDICATION

To the dreamers at heart.

To those who still believe in love, but have decided that belief alone is not enough. To the ones who want more than chemistry, more than hope, and more than a beautiful beginning. To those determined to understand love, build it with intention, repair it with humility, and grow through it with courage. This book is for everyone who refuses to give up on love simply because it is difficult. It is for those who are determined to become successful at love.

This book is dedicated to my spouse, whose steadfast encouragement and belief in me have been a constant source of strength throughout this journey. Your patience, love, and unwavering presence lifted me through moments of doubt and helped me continue forward with confidence. I am deeply grateful for the ways you have supported both me and this work.

To my family, Thomas, Tomika, Carrie, Michelle, Bonnie, and all the aunts and uncles who instilled in me the values of resilience, perseverance, and continuous growth, I offer my profound gratitude. Your sacrifices, wisdom, and unconditional love have provided the foundation upon which I stand today. Every lesson, every word of encouragement, and every gesture of support has served as a guiding force in my pursuit of this meaningful milestone.

To my friends, whose encouragement, honesty, and presence helped sustain me through this work, thank you for reminding me that meaningful progress is never built alone. I especially dedicate this book to Hollie, Miguel, Miguelina, AJ, Kathy, Chai, Omar, and Karra. Each of you has brought wisdom, love, perspective, and light into my life over the years, and your presence has shaped me in ways I will always carry.

This is for you.

ACKNOWLEDGMENTS

Success is often seen as an individual achievement, a pursuit driven by determination and perseverance. Yet I firmly believe that success is never truly singular. It is shaped, nurtured, and sustained by the unwavering support of those who walk beside us.

This book is the result of years of dedication, reflection, learning, and support from those who have guided and encouraged me along the way. I would first like to express my deepest gratitude to the doctors and mentors who provided invaluable guidance: Dr. Rolande Murray, Dr. Rhonda Bohs, Dr. Ethel Perry, Dr. Lois Woods, and Dr. Arcelle Daniels. Your patience, insightful feedback, encouragement, and belief in my work helped shape the ideas that now live within these pages. I also want to express my sincere appreciation to those who offered unwavering support throughout my academic and professional journey. Your words of wisdom, encouragement, and belief in my abilities have been a source of strength and motivation, reminding me to continue moving forward with purpose.

To my incredible P-Power group—Jackson-Poole, Page, Gross, Mason and Perkins—we have been each other's backbone. Our collective energy pushed us forward when the road seemed impossible. We are builders of knowledge, architects of change, and examples of what can happen when determination meets community. This journey was never meant to be walked alone, and I am forever grateful for the laughter, late-night calls, honest conversations, and relentless encouragement. Together, we are creating greatness.

PREFACE

This book began with a question that followed me across several parts of my life: why do intelligent, capable, loving people struggle to build relationships that can survive pressure? I have seen people succeed in business, lead teams, raise families, overcome hardship, and demonstrate remarkable resilience in public life, yet still feel lost when love becomes complicated. They are not careless people. They are not incapable people. Many of them want to love well, communicate better, repair honestly, and create something lasting. Yet wanting a strong relationship and knowing how to build one are not the same thing.

For much of my professional life, I have studied systems. In business, systems reveal why good intentions are not enough. A company can have a strong mission, talented people, loyal customers, and real promise, but if its internal systems are weak, the organization eventually feels the strain. Communication breaks down, assumptions go untested, feedback is ignored, and the organization begins repeating problems it never fully learns from. The same is true in relationships. Love may begin with feeling, but it survives through patterns, structure, repair, adaptation, and the willingness to learn.

The Learning Relationship was written from that central idea. A relationship is not simply an emotional bond between two people. It is a living system shaped by what each person brings, what each person believes, how each person responds under stress, and what both people repeatedly reinforce over time. When a couple does not understand the system they are creating, they may mistake recurring problems for isolated arguments. They may blame personality, timing, chemistry, or incompatibility without ever seeing the pattern beneath the pain. This book is an invitation to look deeper.

The scholarly premise underneath this translation is modest but important: intimate relationships are not reducible to either individual personality or private emotion. They are interactional systems in which feedback, interpretation, reinforcement, and adaptation shape what becomes stable over time. Systems theory provides the language of interdependence; applied behavior analysis provides the language of function and consequence; ACT provides the language of values-based action under emotional pressure. Together, they allow love to be examined without being reduced (von Bertalanffy, 1968; Baer et al., 1968; Hayes et al., 2006).

The framework in these pages draws from business theory, cognitive psychology, behavioral science, and relationship insight. Peter Senge's concept of the learning organization provides one of the major foundations for this work. In business, a learning organization is capable of examining itself, questioning its assumptions, adapting to change, and improving through feedback. This book applies that same logic to intimate relationships, not to make love mechanical, but to make love more conscious. A relationship that can learn is not perfect, but it is capable of becoming wiser over time (Senge, 2006; Argyris & Schön, 1978).

This book also reflects my background in cognitive psychology, applied behavior analysis, business analysis, entrepreneurship, human resources, and relationship research. Those disciplines may appear separate at first, but they often return to the same truth: people and systems are shaped by repeated patterns. What is reinforced becomes more likely. What is avoided becomes more powerful. What is left unnamed begins to organize behavior from beneath awareness. Whether in a business, a family, a marriage, or a personal life, patterns matter because patterns become structure (Skinner, 1953; Baer et al., 1968; Hayes et al., 2006).

The purpose of this book is not to promise that every relationship can be saved. Some relationships are unsafe, one-sided, chronically harmful, or unwilling to change. A learning relationship requires participation, humility, accountability, and enough safety for truth to be spoken and received. This book does not ask anyone to stay where they are being diminished, manipulated, neglected, or harmed. Clarity is not the same as endurance, and understanding a system does not mean remaining inside a system that refuses to become healthy.

At the same time, many relationships do not fail because love was never present. They struggle because love was never given the structure it needed to grow. Two people may care deeply for each other and still repeat patterns neither of them understands. They may want peace but reinforce silence, want closeness but create pressure, want honesty but punish feedback, or want commitment while avoiding the work of repair. This book gives language to those patterns so they can be seen, examined, and changed where change is possible.

The reader should not approach this book as a set of quick fixes. Relationships do not become resilient through slogans, surface techniques, or temporary emotional motivation. They become resilient when people learn to observe themselves, question their assumptions, understand feedback, repair harm, and build shared meaning over time. This work requires honesty. It requires patience. It requires the courage to ask not only whether love is real, but whether the relationship being built can actually support the life being placed upon it.

My hope is that this book helps readers think about love with more precision and more compassion. Precision matters because vague love cannot repair specific patterns. Compassion matters because people often bring old learning into new relationships before they understand what they are carrying. The goal is not to judge people for being unfinished. The goal is to help them become more awake to the ways they participate in what love becomes.

If this book does its work, it will not simply help readers ask, "Do we love each other?" It will help them ask, "What are we building?" It will help them see that the strength of a relationship is not measured only by how powerfully it begins, but by how honestly it learns. Love is not less meaningful because it has structure. It is more likely to last when the people inside it understand how to build, repair, and grow.

TABLE OF CONTENTS

INTRODUCTION

Most people do not lose love because they never felt it. They lose it because they misunderstood what it required.

This is one of the most difficult truths to accept about relationships, because it challenges the story most people inherited long before they ever entered one. We are taught, directly and indirectly, to recognize love by its emotional force. We learn to look for chemistry, ease, attraction, excitement, comfort, and the peculiar sense of recognition that makes another person feel significant before we fully understand why. When those feelings are present, we assume something important has been found. When they are absent, we assume something is missing. For a while, that way of seeing love appears to work.

A relationship begins. There is attention, energy, possibility. The interaction feels different enough to matter. Conversations carry their own momentum. The other person becomes increasingly present in thought, expectation, and imagination. It feels less like something being built and more like something being discovered. Because the feeling is real, the conclusion seems obvious. This must mean something. And it does. But not always what we think it means.

Feeling can tell us that something has been activated. It can tell us that another person matters, that we are drawn toward them, that something in the interaction has emotional significance. What feeling cannot do, at least not by itself, is tell us whether the relationship has the structure required to survive time, stress, misunderstanding, routine, disappointment, and change. That distinction is where many relationships begin to lose clarity.

A relationship can feel meaningful and still be underdeveloped. It can feel natural and still lack the capacity to adapt. It can contain real affection, real attraction, and real commitment, yet still fail to become a system strong enough to hold the lives of the people inside it. This is not because love is false. It is because love is incomplete when it remains only an emotional experience. Love begins in feeling, but it does not survive by feeling alone.

To understand why, we have to change the way we look at relationships. We have to stop seeing them only as private emotional experiences and begin seeing them as living systems.

A system is not just a collection of parts. It is the pattern created by the way those parts interact. In a relationship, the parts are not simply two people. They include each person's history, assumptions, coping strategies, emotional habits, interpretations, values, expectations, and learned responses. They include what is said and what is avoided, what is reinforced and what is punished, what is repeated and what is never examined. Over time, these elements do not remain separate. They organize themselves into patterns. Those patterns become the relationship (von Bertalanffy, 1968; Meadows, 2008).

This is why two intelligent, caring, well-intentioned people can continue to repeat interactions neither of them wants. One withdraws because the conversation feels overwhelming. The other becomes more insistent because withdrawal feels like distance. The increased insistence makes withdrawal feel even more necessary. The withdrawal makes insistence feel even more justified. Each person believes they are responding to the other. In reality, both are participating in a loop. The loop becomes stronger than the moment (Schrodt et al., 2014; Papp et al., 2009).

Eventually, the argument is no longer just about what happened. It is about what has been happening. It carries the weight of prior misunderstandings, unmet expectations, old interpretations, and repeated emotional injuries. By the time the conversation begins, the system is already in motion.

Most couples do not see this. They see the event. They see the tone, the comment, the delayed response, the disagreement, the silence. They focus on the visible disruption and try to resolve it as though it exists by itself. If they can explain the moment, they believe they can fix the problem. But the problem is rarely just the problem. The problem is the pattern beneath it. This book is about learning to see that pattern.

It draws from a simple but demanding idea: relationships do not merely happen between people; they are built through repeated interaction. They are shaped by feedback, reinforced by behavior, distorted by mental models, strained by unexamined expectations, and strengthened only when both individuals become capable of learning within the system they are creating.

The language of systems may seem, at first, too mechanical for something as intimate as love. That reaction is understandable. Love is not a machine. A relationship is not a corporation. A partner is not a process improvement project. The purpose of this book is not to strip love of its humanity or reduce it to a set of sterile principles. It is to take love seriously enough to ask how it actually functions.

Business leaders have long understood that organizations do not succeed on passion alone. A company can have vision, talent, energy, and ambition, yet still fail if its systems are unclear, its assumptions are unexamined, its feedback is ignored, and its people cannot learn together. The same is true in relationships. Attraction may begin the connection. Desire may energize it. Commitment may stabilize it for a time. But without the ability to observe patterns, regulate reactions, revise assumptions, share meaning, and adapt together, the relationship remains vulnerable to forces neither person fully understands. This is where the idea of the learning relationship begins (Senge, 2006; Edmondson, 1999).

A learning relationship is not a perfect relationship. It is not one without conflict, disappointment, or strain. It is not a relationship where both people always communicate well, always respond maturely, or always know what to do. It is a relationship capable of noticing what is happening, making meaning together, adjusting behavior, and becoming more effective over time. Some relationships repeat. Others learn.

The difference is not the absence of difficulty. The difference is what the system does with difficulty once it appears.

In a repeating relationship, conflict becomes evidence. Each disappointment confirms what one person already fears about the other. Each misunderstanding reinforces an existing story. Each emotional reaction narrows the range of possible responses. The relationship becomes increasingly organized around protection, prediction, and defense. The same issues return, often in different forms, because the underlying pattern has not changed.

In a learning relationship, difficulty becomes information. Not because it stops hurting, and not because everything can be calmly analyzed in the moment, but because both individuals develop the capacity to step back and ask a different kind of question. Not simply, "Who caused this?" but, "What is happening between us that keeps producing this result?" Not simply, "Why did you do that?" but, "What did each of us bring into this moment?" Not simply, "How do we stop fighting?" but, "What pattern are we reinforcing, and what would it require to build a different one?" This shift changes the entire emotional landscape of the relationship.

Blame begins to lose its authority. Not because accountability disappears, but because accountability expands. Each person is still responsible for their behavior, their words, their choices, and their impact. But they also become responsible for understanding how those behaviors participate in a larger system. The question is no longer limited to what one person did. It becomes how both people are shaping what happens next. That is a more difficult question. It is also a more useful one.

Most people are more practiced at defending themselves than observing themselves. This is not a moral failure. It is a human pattern. The mind protects its own interpretations. It looks for confirmation. It assigns meaning quickly, especially under stress. A delayed response becomes indifference. A short answer becomes rejection. A disagreement becomes incompatibility. Once meaning is assigned, emotion follows. Once emotion intensifies, behavior begins to organize around it. By the time people react, they often believe they are responding to reality. More often, they are responding to the meaning their mind has placed on reality (Tversky & Kahneman, 1974; Kahneman, 2011; Bradbury & Fincham, 1990).

This is why mental models' matter. Every person enters love with invisible rules about what closeness should look like, what conflict means, what silence indicates, what loyalty requires, what safety feels like, and what another person should know without being told. These rules are rarely written down. They are absorbed through family, culture, previous relationships, injury, longing, and survival. They become so familiar that they feel like truth. Then two people enter a relationship with different invisible rules and wonder why love becomes difficult. (Senge, 2006; Bradbury & Fincham, 1990).

They may use the same words and mean entirely different things. Both may value communication, but one defines communication as frequent emotional sharing while the other defines it as direct discussion when something needs to be solved. Both may value commitment, but one experiences commitment as emotional reassurance while the other expresses it through reliability and responsibility. Both may value respect, but one sees respect as honesty without avoidance while the other sees it as restraint without confrontation. The value is shared. The operating definition is not.

This is where many relationships begin to strain. Not because the people are incompatible in some absolute sense, but because the system has not learned how to translate, align, and adapt. What feels like opposition may actually be misalignment. What feels like indifference may actually be a different model of care. What feels like criticism may actually be an unskilled attempt at repair. What feels like distance may actually be self-protection.

None of this excuse's harmful behavior. Understanding a system does not mean tolerating what damages you. It does not mean accepting neglect, betrayal, contempt, manipulation, or emotional irresponsibility. Clarity is not the same as permission. In some relationships, seeing the system clearly reveals what must change. In others, it reveals what cannot safely continue. But even then, clarity matters.

A person who understands relationships as systems leaves with different knowledge than a person who only leaves with pain. They begin to recognize the patterns they participated in, the assumptions they carried, the signals they ignored, and the forms of love they mistook for structure. They become less likely to repeat the same architecture with a different person. That is one of the central aims of this book.

Not simply to help readers preserve a relationship, but to help them understand what they are building, what they are repeating, and what their relationship is becoming over time. This requires a different relationship with the self.

It is tempting to think that relational change begins with getting the other person to understand. Sometimes that is necessary. But the first unavoidable task is personal mastery. Not control. Not suppression. Not a polished performance of emotional maturity. Personal mastery is the capacity to observe yourself while you are activated, to recognize the space between feeling and action, to question the interpretation that arrived automatically, and to choose a response that serves the relationship rather than simply relieving the discomfort of the moment. This is harder than it sounds (Senge, 2006; Hayes et al., 2006; Gross, 1998).

Under stress, people tend to become loyal to their old patterns. They withdraw, pursue, explain, defend, collapse, criticize, appease, shut down, or escalate. These responses may not be effective, but they are familiar. Familiarity has a strange authority in the nervous system. It can make an old reaction feel safer than a better one (Lazarus & Folkman, 1984; Randall & Bodenmann, 2009).

Personal mastery asks for something different. It asks you to become someone who can stay present long enough to see what is happening before you become consumed by it. It asks you to stop treating your first reaction as your final truth. It asks you to take responsibility for the version of yourself that enters the system when the relationship becomes difficult. This does not mean you are responsible for everything that happens. It means you are responsible for what you bring into what happens.

That distinction will appear throughout this book because it is essential. Relationships are never shaped by one person alone, but every person shapes the relationship. What you bring becomes part of what you build. Your unexamined assumptions, your emotional habits, your avoidance, your urgency, your fear of rejection, your need for control, your discomfort with vulnerability, your hunger for reassurance, your silence, your timing, your tone, your willingness or unwillingness to repair—all of it enters the system. The relationship has to work with what is actually present, not with what either person intended to bring. This is why intention is not enough.

Many people intend to love well. They intend to be patient, honest, supportive, generous, and loyal. But relationships are not sustained by intention in the abstract. They are sustained by patterns of behavior under real conditions. Who you are when you are calm matters. Who you become when you are threatened matters more.

The same is true for the relationship itself. A couple is not defined by how they feel when things are easy. They are defined by how they function when the conditions change. Stress reveals the system. Disappointment reveals the system. Conflict reveals the system. Routine reveals the system. Time reveals the system. This is not a cynical view of love. It is a respectful one.

It refuses to treat love as fragile magic that must remain unexamined in order to survive. It assumes that love can withstand clarity. More than that, it assumes love requires clarity. The relationships that endure are not those that avoid pressure. They are those that develop the capacity to respond to pressure without losing their structure. That capacity is built.

It is built through awareness, through repetition, through repair, through feedback, through shared meaning, through the willingness to revise what no longer works. It is built when two people stop asking only whether they love each other and begin asking whether the system they are creating can actually support the life they are trying to live. This book is organized around that movement.

It begins with the illusion, because most people cannot build differently until they understand the story they inherited. The early chapters examine why love is so often mistaken for feeling, why connection is confused with compatibility, and why the first signs of strain are misunderstood. They also look at what each person brings into the relationship before the relationship ever begins: the invisible operating system of values, assumptions, habits, and patterns that quietly shape what gets built.

From there, the book turns toward the system itself. It examines how relationships form patterns, how feedback loops develop, how partners reinforce each other's behavior without realizing it, and why blame feels satisfying but rarely produces lasting change. It then moves inward, into personal mastery and mental models, because no one can participate wisely in a system they are unwilling to examine within themselves.

The middle of the book follows the pattern of love over time. It looks at the cycle that moves relationships from early intensity into exposure, strain, confusion, and choice. It explores the shift from "me" to "us," a shift many couples assume will happen naturally but often never intentionally build. It asks what love is actually made of once fantasy, novelty, and emotional intensity are no longer sufficient to explain what is happening.

The final section introduces the learning relationship. This is where the central premise becomes practical. A relationship that can learn is one that can use conflict as information, feedback as guidance, repair as structure, and strategy as a form of care. It does not become cold or mechanical by becoming intentional. It becomes more capable. It becomes less dependent on emotional accident and more grounded in shared awareness. Strategic love is not love without feeling. It is love with direction (Hayes et al., 2012; Senge, 2006).

It is the difference between hoping the relationship will hold and building the conditions that allow it to hold. It is the difference between reacting to drift after it has created distance and noticing the early signals that the system needs attention. It is the difference between repeating inherited patterns and creating new ones with enough consistency that the relationship begins to change.

There is no promise here that every relationship can or should be saved. Some relationships are too damaged, too unsafe, too one-sided, or too unwilling to become learning systems. A relationship cannot learn if only one person is willing to observe, adjust, and repair. A system requires participation. It requires enough humility from both people to see what they have helped create and enough responsibility to change what they continue to reinforce. But whether a relationship continues or ends, the way it is understood matters.

When you see love only as feeling, you are left interpreting every change in feeling as evidence. When you see love as a system, you begin to understand that change is not always loss. Sometimes it is exposure. Sometimes it is information. Sometimes it is the first visible sign that the relationship has reached the limits of its current structure and must either learn or repeat. That is the invitation of this book.

Not to abandon romance, but to mature it. Not to distrust feeling, but to stop asking feeling to do the work of structure. Not to turn love into a business, but to borrow from systems, learning, behavior, and psychology what love has always needed but rarely been taught to use. Love is not less meaningful because it has patterns. It is more workable because it has patterns.

And once those patterns can be seen, they can be understood. Once they can be understood, they can be changed. Once they can be changed, love becomes something more than something that happened to you. It becomes something you can build.

PART I
THE ILLUSION

Before a relationship becomes difficult, it usually feels understandable.

This is part of what makes love so convincing in the beginning. It does not arrive as a system to be studied. It arrives as an experience to be felt. It moves through attention, attraction, ease, longing, curiosity, and the quiet belief that something meaningful has begun. Most people do not enter love by asking how the relationship will function under stress, how conflict will be handled, what patterns each person brings, or whether the structure being formed can sustain the life eventually placed upon it. They enter through feeling. And because the feeling is real, they assume the understanding is real as well. That assumption is the first illusion.

The illusion is not that love is false. It is not that chemistry is meaningless, attraction is shallow, or emotional connection should be distrusted. The illusion is subtler than that. It is the belief that the experience of love is the same as the capacity for relationship. It is the belief that because something feels significant, it is therefore prepared to become stable. It is the belief that if two people feel strongly enough, the rest will somehow organize itself around the feeling.

For a time, that belief appears to work. Early love often carries its own momentum. The relationship seems to move before either person has to direct it. Attention comes easily. Communication feels natural. Differences are softened by curiosity. Uncertainty is absorbed by hope. The relationship feels less like something being built and more like something being revealed.

But what feels effortless in the beginning is not always evidence of strength. Often, it is evidence of conditions that have not yet changed.

In the early stage, the relationship is protected from much of what will eventually test it. There are fewer shared responsibilities, fewer accumulated disappointments, fewer moments where values collide, fewer demands on time, attention, money, energy, patience, and emotional regulation. Each person is still meeting the other in a narrow range of conditions. They are not being dishonest. They are being incomplete, because no relationship reveals the whole of either person at the beginning. The beginning gives information. It does not give the whole truth.

Part I begins there, with the story most people inherit about love and the confusion that follows when that story stops explaining what is happening. The chapters in this section examine the illusion of love as it is commonly understood: love as emotional certainty, love as compatibility, love as something found rather than built, love as a feeling strong enough to carry what only structure can sustain.

Chapter 1, "The Illusion of Love," addresses the inherited story directly. It explores how people learn to recognize love through feeling, why early emotional intensity becomes mistaken for evidence, and how connection can create the appearance of compatibility before the relationship has been tested. It also introduces the first major shift in the book: the move from seeing love as an emotional event to seeing it as something that must eventually function under real conditions.

Chapter 2, "What You Bring Into Love," turns the attention inward. Once the illusion of love as pure discovery begins to weaken, another truth becomes visible: no one enters a relationship empty-handed. Each person brings history, assumptions, fears, coping strategies, values, patterns, habits, and ways of assigning meaning. These do not wait outside the relationship. They become part of it. What you bring into love becomes part of what love has to work with.

The purpose of this first part is not to make the reader suspicious of love. It is to make love more visible. Illusions are not always lies. Sometimes they are partial truths that have been allowed to stand in for the whole. The feeling of love may be real. The connection may be real. The hope may be real. But none of those realities, by themselves, tell us whether the relationship has the structure, awareness, and adaptive capacity required to endure. Before love can be built differently, it has to be seen differently. That is where this book begins.

CHAPTER ONE

THE ILLUSION OF LOVE

What We Were Told, What We Believed, and Why It Doesn't Work

There is a version of love most people carry long before they ever understand what a relationship requires. It does not come from maturity. It does not come from sustained partnership. It does not come from the ordinary experience of trying to build a life with another person under real conditions. It comes from somewhere earlier, somewhere more impressionable, somewhere so familiar that it rarely feels like an idea at all. It comes from the stories.

Not only the obvious ones. Not only the films, songs, novels, weddings, family myths, and cultural scripts that taught us how love was supposed to look. It comes from the way love was described without being explained, celebrated without being examined, and treated as though its presence should naturally solve what human beings themselves had never learned how to build.

Somewhere along the way, love became something that was supposed to happen to us. It was supposed to arrive. It was supposed to feel unmistakable. It was supposed to find us, move us, claim us, and reveal something essential about who we were and who we were meant to be with. If it felt right, then everything else would follow.

No one had to say it that plainly. The message was carried in implication. If it is right, it will work. If it is meant to be, it will last. If you love each other enough, you will figure it out. If the connection is real, the relationship will know how to become what it needs to become.

These ideas sound harmless when they are spoken gently. They can even sound wise. But ideas that feel true before they have been tested are often the most powerful, because they shape perception before evidence ever has a chance to intervene.

At first, the story appears to hold. You meet someone. The interaction feels different enough to matter. There is ease, interest, attraction, curiosity, and some form of recognition that makes the person stand apart from the rest of ordinary life. The conversation moves without strain. Time changes its pace. The other person begins to occupy more mental space than expected. There is a sense of unfolding, as if something is happening on its own.

In that moment, without realizing it, you begin comparing the experience to the version of love you have been carrying. Not consciously, perhaps not even deliberately, but automatically. Does this feel right? Is this what it is supposed to feel like? Is this what I have been waiting for?

The answers do not usually arrive through careful thought. They arrive through emotion. The feeling becomes the evidence. If the feeling is strong enough, the conclusion begins to form before the relationship has been tested. This must mean something. And it does. But not always what we think it means.

Feeling can tell us that something has been activated. It can tell us that another person matters, that the interaction has emotional significance, that something in us is responding. It can draw our attention toward possibility. What feeling cannot do, at least not by itself, is tell us whether the relationship has the structure required to survive disappointment, routine, stress, conflict, ambiguity, growth, injury, repair, and time. That distinction is where many relationships begin to lose clarity.

A relationship can feel meaningful and still be underdeveloped. It can feel natural and still lack the capacity to adapt. It can contain real affection, real attraction, real hope, and real commitment, yet still fail to become strong enough to hold the lives of the people inside it. This is not because the love was false. It is because love is incomplete when it remains only an emotional experience. Love begins in feeling, but it does not survive by feeling alone.

Most people do not lose love because they never felt it. They lose it because they misunderstood what the feeling was capable of doing. They expected love to carry responsibilities that feeling was never designed to carry. They expected connection to substitute for compatibility, intention to substitute for behavior, chemistry to substitute for structure, and hope to substitute for the disciplined work of learning how the relationship actually functions. This misunderstanding is not a personal failure. It is an inherited framework.

The inherited framework tells us to look for signs. Signs of interest. Signs of chemistry. Signs of emotional availability. Signs that someone sees us, chooses us, values us, and makes us feel the way we imagined love would feel. The framework is not entirely wrong. These signs matter. A relationship without warmth, desire, connection, and emotional resonance is not likely to become a fulfilling partnership. But the framework becomes dangerous when those signs are mistaken for the whole structure. Connection is not the same as compatibility. Intensity is not the same as depth. Comfort is not the same as safety. Desire is not the same as readiness. Commitment is not the same as capacity (Sternberg, 1986; Hazan & Shaver, 1987).

These distinctions rarely matter in the beginning because the beginning protects us from needing them. Early love often occurs in conditions that make the relationship appear more functional than it has actually had to become. There are fewer shared burdens. There are fewer consequences attached to misunderstanding. There are fewer routines, fewer competing obligations, fewer accumulated injuries, and fewer opportunities for disappointment to reveal how two people actually respond when reality interrupts the story.

In the beginning, much of the relationship exists in a selective environment. Each person is showing a version of themselves that is not false, but not complete. They are attentive because attention is easy to offer when novelty is high. They are curious because there is still so much to discover. They are flexible because the relationship has not yet required much sacrifice. They are patient because the system has not yet been stressed. Nothing has been tested. Not really. And because nothing has been tested, little has been proven.

Yet the absence of conflict is often interpreted as evidence of strength. The lack of friction feels like compatibility. The ease of communication feels like alignment. The emotional momentum feels like stability. The relationship is experienced as effortless, and effortlessness is treated as confirmation that something rare and durable has been found.

This is one of the earliest illusions of love: that what feels easy at the beginning will remain easy if the relationship is right.

But ease in the beginning is often a function of conditions, not capacity. A system that has not been placed under pressure cannot reveal how well it will perform under pressure. Two people can communicate beautifully when nothing threatens them. They can feel deeply connected when neither has had to disappoint the other. They can appear emotionally generous when no one has asked for something difficult, inconvenient, or frightening. They can seem aligned when the relationship has not yet required decisions that expose competing values. The beginning tells us something. It does not tell us everything.

Over time, the protected environment begins to change. This does not always happen dramatically. Often, it begins in small deviations from what once felt consistent. A message takes longer to receive a response. A conversation does not move with the same ease. A tone feels slightly altered. A need is expressed and not met in the expected way. A misunderstanding lingers. A small disappointment feels larger than it should. Nothing catastrophic has happened. Still, something feels different. This is where many people begin to ask the wrong question. They ask, "What happened to the feeling?"

The question seems natural because the feeling was treated as the foundation. If the relationship felt certain before and feels uncertain now, then the feeling appears to be the thing that has changed. If the feeling has changed, then the relationship itself must be changing. If the relationship is changing, then perhaps something is wrong. But what if the feeling was never the foundation? What if it was only the beginning?

That possibility is harder to accept because it requires a different relationship with love. It requires us to stop treating emotional intensity as proof of relational strength. It requires us to understand that the early feeling of love is not a completed structure. It is an activation. It brings energy, movement, attention, and possibility. It opens the door. It does not build the house. The emotional fallacy begins when we ask feeling to do the work of understanding.

Emotion is essential to love, but it is not a reliable instrument for measuring the whole relationship. Emotion is responsive. It shifts with context, memory, expectation, fatigue, stress, interpretation, and previous injury. What feels clear in one moment can feel uncertain in another. What feels safe at the beginning can feel exposed later. What feels intense in early connection can quiet into something less dramatic but potentially more stable, if the relationship knows how to develop. The problem is not that emotion changes. The problem is that people often interpret change in emotion as evidence of decline.

When early intensity settles, many people assume something has been lost. They compare the present relationship to the earlier version and conclude that the difference must signal a problem. They try to recover the feeling, return to the beginning, or recreate the conditions that once made love feel effortless.

But a relationship cannot live indefinitely in its beginning. The beginning is not meant to be permanent. It is meant to initiate movement into something more developed.

A mature relationship is not a preserved early-stage romance. It is a system that has learned how to remain connected after the first conditions have changed. It has learned how to respond to stress, how to clarify expectations, how to repair injury, how to coordinate under pressure, how to revise assumptions, and how to keep becoming more honest without becoming less loving. That kind of relationship does not emerge by accident. It has to be built.

The difficulty is that many people enter relationships with a deep longing to be loved but very little understanding of what love requires once the longing is answered. They know how they want to feel. They know what they hope the other person will provide. They may even know what kind of life they want to create. But they have not always examined the internal systems they bring with them: the assumptions, interpretations, emotional habits, fears, defenses, values, and behavioral patterns that will become part of the relationship whether they acknowledge them or not. This is why love can feel right and still fail. The feeling reflects one layer of the relationship. The outcome reflects the system.

A system is not just a collection of parts. It is the pattern created by the way those parts interact. In a relationship, the parts are not simply two people. They include each person's history, beliefs, emotional responses, coping strategies, expectations, communication style, family conditioning, prior wounds, unspoken rules, and ways of assigning meaning. These elements do not remain separate. They interact. They reinforce each other. They organize themselves into patterns. Those patterns become the relationship (von Bertalanffy, 1968; Meadows, 2008).

This is why two people can care deeply about each other and still repeat interactions neither of them wants. One person feels distance and reaches for reassurance. The other feels pressure and withdraws. The withdrawal increases the first person's fear. The increased pursuit deepens the second person's need for space. Each person believes they are responding to the other. In reality, both are participating in a loop. The loop becomes stronger than the moment (Schrodt et al., 2014; Candel & Turliuc, 2019).

Eventually, the conflict is no longer about the delayed response, the tone, the forgotten errand, the missed signal, or the disagreement at hand. The present event carries the weight of previous events. The current reaction contains old interpretations. The argument feels larger than the topic because it is connected to a pattern that has been building over time.

From inside the relationship, this can be bewildering. Two people find themselves in a conflict that seems disproportionate to the situation. Afterward, they may review the details and still struggle to explain why things escalated. The event itself does not contain enough information to make sense of the reaction. That is because the event is not the whole story. The pattern beneath it is.

Most people are trained to look at the event. What did they say? Why did they say it that way? Why did I react like that? Who started it? Who was wrong? Who needs to apologize? These questions may matter, but they rarely go far enough. They keep attention fixed on the surface of the relationship, where problems appear as isolated incidents rather than expressions of a deeper structure.

If the relationship is understood only through events, the solution will always be limited. People will try to fix the argument instead of understanding the loop. They will try to clarify the sentence instead of examining the assumptions beneath it. They will try to restore the feeling instead of building the structure that would allow the relationship to remain stable when the feeling changes. This is why blame is so tempting.

Blame simplifies complexity. It gives the mind somewhere to land. If one person caused the problem, then one person can correct it. If one person is wrong, the other can feel justified. Blame creates an immediate sense of order in a situation that feels emotionally disorganized. But blame rarely changes the system.

It may identify a behavior that matters. It may point toward accountability that is necessary. But when blame becomes the primary framework, it narrows attention. It isolates one person's action from the interaction that produced and reinforced it. It turns the relationship into a contest of perspectives, where each person defends their version of reality instead of examining how both versions are participating in a shared pattern.

Moving beyond blame does not mean abandoning accountability. Accountability is essential. Harmful behavior must be named. Avoidance, contempt, dishonesty, manipulation, neglect, betrayal, and emotional irresponsibility cannot be hidden behind the language of systems. Understanding the pattern does not excuse the behavior. But accountability becomes more useful when it is placed inside the pattern.

The question is not only, "What did you do?" It is also, "How did we get here?" Not only, "Who is responsible for this moment?" but, "What have we been reinforcing that made this moment more likely?" Not only, "How do we stop this fight?" but, "What kind of relationship are we repeatedly creating through the way we respond to each other?"

These questions require more maturity than blame because they ask each person to remain present without collapsing into self-defense. They require the ability to examine one's own role without turning every problem inward as shame. They require enough emotional steadiness to see that responsibility is not the same as fault. Fault looks backward and searches for a single cause. Responsibility looks forward and asks what must change.

The first signs that something is off in a relationship are often invitations into this deeper form of responsibility. Unfortunately, they are usually misread. A couple notices distance and assumes the solution is to get back to closeness. They notice conflict and assume the solution is to argue less. They notice uncertainty and assume the solution is to force reassurance. These responses are understandable, but they often attempt to restore a prior emotional state rather than understand the emerging structure. The moment something feels off is not always a sign that love is ending. Sometimes it is the first sign that the relationship has reached the limits of its current design.

That limit may appear through stress. Stress is one of the clearest tests of a relationship because it removes the conditions that made connection easy. Work demands increase. Money becomes complicated. Family obligations intrude. Health changes. Children arrive. Responsibilities multiply. Time becomes less available. Rest becomes less consistent. The relationship is no longer protected by novelty and selective attention. It is now operating inside life. This is where partnership reveals itself.

There is a common assumption that two people become a team because they love each other or because they have chosen each other. In reality, partnership does not emerge automatically from affection or commitment. Two people can be deeply connected and still respond to stress as separate individuals. They may live together, plan together, share responsibilities, and still cope alone inside the relationship.

One withdraws because they learned long ago to handle pressure privately. The other feels shut out because closeness, for them, means being included in the inner experience. One tries to solve the problem quickly because uncertainty feels unsafe. The other slows down because speed feels overwhelming. One needs verbal reassurance. The other offers practical support. Both may be trying. Both may be loving. But the system remains uncoordinated. The relationship is not lacking feeling. It is lacking integration.

This distinction matters. Many relationships do not struggle because the people involved do not care. They struggle because caring has not become coordinated action. Affection has not become shared process. Commitment has not become a reliable way of responding to stress. The relationship exists, but it does not yet function as a unified system.

Under stress, people tend to return to the coping strategies that existed before the relationship. These strategies are familiar because they were built earlier. They may have been necessary. They may have helped the person survive conflict, uncertainty, criticism, emotional absence, or instability. But what protected a person in one environment may strain a relationship in another.

A person who learned to become self-sufficient may not know how to let another person participate in their burden. A person who learned to monitor emotional shifts may interpret every change in tone as danger. A person who learned that needs were ignored may express them with urgency that overwhelms the other. A person who learned that conflict leads to rupture may disappear emotionally at the first sign of tension. These responses are not random. They are learned. And because they are learned, they enter the relationship as part of the system.

This is one of the reasons loves feels so confusing. People often believe they are reacting to what is happening now, when they are also reacting through what they have learned before. A delayed response is not only a delayed response. It may become abandonment, disrespect, rejection, or proof that the relationship is changing. A request is not only a request. It may become criticism, control, pressure, or evidence that nothing is ever enough. The present moment becomes crowded with old meaning.

Once meaning is assigned, emotion follows. Once emotion intensifies, behavior organizes around it. The person who feels rejected may protest, withdraw, or test the other person's care. The person who feels criticized may defend, shut down, or counterattack. Neither person is responding to the event alone. Each is responding to the meaning the mind has attached to the event. This is why awareness is the first real turning point (Lazarus & Folkman, 1984; Bradbury & Fincham, 1990).

Awareness rarely arrives as a dramatic revelation. More often, it begins as a pause. A slight distance between what happened and what you assume it means. A moment in which you notice that your reaction feels familiar, perhaps too familiar. A recognition that this conflict has appeared before, even if the details are different. A question that interrupts the automatic story. What is actually happening here? That question is small, but it changes the direction of the relationship.

Before awareness, the relationship is experienced primarily from inside the reaction. Feelings seem self-evident. Interpretations feel like facts. The other person's behavior appears to be the obvious cause of one's response. After awareness begins, the same interaction becomes more layered. There is the event, the interpretation, the emotion, the behavior, and the pattern that connects them. This does not make the relationship easier. It makes it clearer.

Clarity is not always comfortable. In fact, the first stage of clarity often feels destabilizing because it removes the simplicity that blame and fantasy once provided. It becomes harder to say, "This is all their fault." It becomes harder to say, "If we loved each other, this would not be happening." It becomes harder to believe that the early feeling should have protected the relationship from the need to grow. But clarity also creates possibility.

If the relationship is shaped by patterns, then those patterns can be observed. If they can be observed, they can be understood. If they can be understood, they can be changed, provided both people are willing and the relationship is safe enough to support that change. This is where the illusion of love begins to give way to something more useful. The illusion says love should feel right and then keep feeling right if it is real. Awareness says love may feel right at the beginning, but it must learn how to function over time. The illusion says connection means compatibility.

Awareness says connection opens the door, but compatibility is revealed through stress, difference, repair, and repeated behavior. The illusion says conflict means something is wrong. Awareness says conflict often reveals the structure that has been operating beneath the surface. The illusion says the right person will make love easier. Awareness says the right relationship still requires a system capable of learning.

This does not make love less meaningful. It makes love more honest. It allows us to stop treating difficulty as evidence that the relationship was never real and start asking whether the relationship has developed the capacity required for what it is now facing.

Some relationships will not have that capacity. Some will be unwilling to build it. Some will reveal patterns that are too damaging, too unsafe, or too one-sided to continue. Seeing love as a system does not mean every relationship should be preserved. It means the relationship should be understood accurately enough that choices are made from clarity rather than illusion. There is dignity in that kind of clarity.

A person who understands only the feeling may leave a relationship with heartbreak and confusion. A person who understands the system may leave with grief, but also with knowledge. They may see the assumptions they carried, the patterns they repeated, the signs they dismissed, the behaviors they tolerated, the ways they contributed, and the kinds of structure they will need to build differently in the future.

The goal is not to make love clinical. It is not to strip away romance, tenderness, desire, or mystery. Love should still move us. It should still soften parts of us. It should still create moments that cannot be reduced to a framework. But love also deserves more than mythology. It deserves the kind of attention we give to things we genuinely want to last. To take love seriously is to stop expecting it to survive on emotional force alone.

It is to ask what the relationship is becoming through repeated interaction. It is to ask what is being reinforced, what is being avoided, what is being misunderstood, and what is being built without being named. It is to recognize that two people are not only having a relationship. They are creating one, moment by moment, response by response, pattern by pattern. The beginning of awareness is the end of passivity.

Once you see the relationship as something being shaped, you can no longer relate to it only as something happening to you. You become implicated in it. Not blamed for all of it. Not responsible for the other person's behavior. Not obligated to save what cannot or should not be saved. But implicated in the patterns you reinforce, the meanings you assign, the responses you repeat, and the version of yourself you bring into the system. That is a heavier responsibility than the inherited story promised. It is also more freeing.

Because if love is only something that happens, then you can only hope it happens correctly. You can only hope you find the right person, feel the right feeling, avoid the wrong conflict, and somehow arrive at lasting partnership through a combination of chemistry, timing, and luck.

But if love is also something that is built, then it becomes workable. Not controllable in every way. Not guaranteed. Not immune to loss. But workable. It can be observed. It can be strengthened. It can be repaired when the conditions allow repair. It can become wiser than the people were when they first entered it. That is where the illusion ends. Not with the rejection of love, but with a more mature understanding of what love requires. Love is not less real because it needs structure. It is more likely to endure when it has one.

CHAPTER TWO

WHAT YOU BRING INTO LOVE

Why the Relationship Begins Before the Relationship Begins

Most people enter love believing they are looking for someone.

They are looking for connection, companionship, affection, loyalty, attraction, understanding, safety, and a future that feels more meaningful because another person is in it. They are looking for someone who fits, someone who sees them, someone whose presence changes the emotional texture of ordinary life. The language of searching is so familiar that it rarely feels incomplete. People speak of finding love, finding the right person, finding someone who makes sense after so many others did not.

There is truth in that language. The person you choose matters. Their character matters. Their emotional capacity matters. Their honesty, maturity, consistency, values, and ability to repair matter. Love is not built in abstraction. It is built with someone, and the qualities of that someone will shape the relationship in profound ways. But there is another side of the equation that receives far less attention. You are not only looking for love. You are bringing something into it.

Before the first conversation deepens, before the first attachment forms, before the relationship has a name, you already arrive with a history. You bring assumptions about closeness, conflict, commitment, and care. You bring expectations you may never have spoken aloud. You bring patterns of communication, emotional habits, defensive strategies, private fears, family lessons, cultural stories, and interpretations that feel so natural you may mistake them for reality itself.

You bring the way you learned to ask for what you need, or the way you learned not to ask. You bring the way you respond when someone disappoints you. You bring the way you interpret silence, the way you experience distance, the way you manage uncertainty, and the way you behave when you feel misunderstood. You bring the version of yourself that appears when love is easy, and the version that appears when love becomes demanding. All of this enters the relationship with you. It does not wait outside the door.

This is one of the most important truths about partnership: the relationship begins before the relationship begins. It begins in the patterns each person has already built, the beliefs each person has already absorbed, and the emotional strategies each person has already practiced. By the time two people meet, both are carrying material that will eventually become part of the system they create together.

At the beginning, that material may not be visible. Early connection often gives the impression that two people are meeting each other in the present, free from the weight of what came before. The conversation feels immediate. The attraction feels current. The attention feels alive. It seems as though the relationship is being formed entirely by what is happening now. But no one meets only in the present.

Each person meets through memory, expectation, longing, and learning. Each person interprets the other through a private architecture of meaning. One person's warmth may feel safe because it resembles something familiar. Another person's independence may feel attractive because it creates a sense of challenge. Someone's attention may feel healing because it answers an old absence. Someone's steadiness may feel foreign because chaos has been mistaken for intensity for too long. The present moment is real, but it is never empty (Bowlby, 1969; Ainsworth et al., 1978; Hazan & Shaver, 1987).

This is why people can be surprised by themselves in relationships. They may believe they are calm, generous, patient, and emotionally reasonable until the relationship touches a pattern that has never been tested in that way. They may believe they are independent until they feel the anxiety of uncertain attachment.

They may believe they are open until intimacy requires them to reveal what they have learned to protect. They may believe they value communication until a difficult conversation threatens their sense of control. The relationship does not always create these reactions. Often, it reveals them.

This is not a reason for shame. It is a reason for accuracy. Many of the patterns' people bring into love were formed long before they had the language to understand them. Some were learned in families where conflict was avoided, exaggerated, punished, or unresolved. Some were shaped by relationships where needs were dismissed, boundaries were crossed, or affection was inconsistent. Some were formed through success, not trauma, because independence, control, charm, achievement, or emotional restraint may have been rewarded in other areas of life. A pattern does not need to be pathological to become relationally significant. It only needs to be repeated.

When a relationship begins, these patterns enter quietly. They do not usually announce themselves as problems. They appear as preferences, instincts, reactions, and familiar ways of making sense of things. A person may say, "I just need space," without recognizing that space has become their automatic response to vulnerability. Another may say, "I just need reassurance," without recognizing that reassurance has become the only way they know how to regulate uncertainty. One may say, "I do not like conflict," when what they mean is that disagreement feels unsafe. Another may say, "I am just being honest," when honesty has become a way to discharge discomfort without considering impact. These responses may feel natural. That does not mean they are neutral.

What you bring into love becomes part of what love has to work with. This is where the romantic story begins to narrow. It tells us to focus on the person we find, as though the right person will automatically call forth the best version of us. Sometimes a good relationship does invite growth. Sometimes another person's steadiness, patience, clarity, and care create conditions where we become more regulated, more honest, and more capable of intimacy. But even the healthiest relationship cannot permanently compensate for patterns we refuse to examine. The right person does not erase the self you bring. The right person still has to live with it.

That is where many relationships begin to strain. Not because love is absent, but because the people inside the relationship are asking love to carry what their own development has not yet addressed. They want closeness, but they have not learned how to remain present when closeness makes them feel exposed. They want honesty, but they have not learned how to hear discomfort without defending. They want emotional safety, but they have not learned how to communicate needs without testing, accusing, withdrawing, or controlling. They want trust, but they continue to behave from the fear that trust will not be safe. Desire is not the same as readiness. This distinction is simple, but it changes everything.

Desire tells you what you want. Readiness tells you what you can sustain. Desire moves toward connection. Readiness determines what happens when that connection requires consistency, patience, repair, restraint, humility, and change.

Desire may be sincere and still outpace capacity. A person can deeply want a stable relationship and still lack the patterns required to help create one. They can want intimacy and still resist vulnerability. They can want commitment and still disappear emotionally when pressure rises. They can want peace and still bring a nervous system organized around threat. Most people confuse wanting love with being prepared for love.

The confusion is understandable. Wanting is easy to recognize. It has emotional force. It creates movement. It feels convincing because it is felt directly. Readiness is harder to see because it is not revealed in longing. It is revealed in function. It shows itself in what a person does repeatedly, especially when the relationship becomes difficult.

Readiness is visible in how someone handles disappointment. It is visible in whether they can tell the truth without becoming cruel, hear the truth without collapsing, and repair harm without reducing the apology to a performance of regret. It is visible in whether they can stay engaged when discomfort rises, whether they can respect a boundary without experiencing it as rejection, whether they can ask for reassurance without making the other person responsible for every fear they carry. Readiness is not perfection. It is developed capacity.

That capacity is often uneven. A person may be highly capable in one area and underdeveloped in another. They may be responsible, loyal, and dependable, yet emotionally unavailable when vulnerability is required. They may be expressive, affectionate, and generous, yet reactive when they feel uncertain. They may be thoughtful and intelligent, yet unable to recognize the assumptions shaping their behavior. They may have built a successful career, managed teams, raised children, endured hardship, and still find themselves repeating the same relational pattern in moments of stress. Human development is not uniform.

This is why love exposes people differently than other parts of life. A person can appear composed in public and become defensive in private. They can be admired professionally and struggle relationally. They can manage complexity at work and avoid complexity at home. They can solve problems for others and remain unable to observe the problems they help create with the person closest to them. Relationships reveal the parts of us that are difficult to see from a distance (Candel & Turliuc, 2019; Daks & Rogge, 2020).

They do this because relationships place our patterns in constant interaction with another person's patterns. What we bring is no longer theoretical. It produces effects. Our timing affects someone else's nervous system. Our silence becomes someone else's uncertainty. Our criticism becomes someone else's guardedness. Our avoidance becomes someone else's pursuit. Our urgency becomes someone else's pressure. Our fear becomes part of the atmosphere. This is where the idea of the self as a product becomes useful, if it is understood carefully.

In business, a product is not judged by intention. It is judged by performance under real conditions. A product may have a compelling story, attractive design, strong potential, and enthusiastic early interest, but none of those things determine whether it can endure use, pressure, variation, and time. Eventually, the product has to work. It has to function beyond presentation. It has to do what it claims to do when the environment is not ideal. The same principle applies to what we offer in relationships.

Not because people are objects, brands, or commodities. They are not. A human being is never reducible to performance. But the metaphor clarifies something that romance often obscures: what you believe you offer is not always what another person experiences. Your intention may be love, but your pattern may feel inconsistent. Your desire may be closeness, but your behavior may create distance. Your self-image may be honest, but your communication may feel unsafe. Your commitment may be real, but your reliability under stress may be uneven. The relationship is not sustained by what you meant to offer. It is sustained by what repeatedly shows up.

This is a difficult distinction because most people experience themselves through intention. You know what you meant. You know what you hoped to communicate. You know the private explanation behind your behavior. You know that you did not intend to hurt, dismiss, pressure, or disappoint. Because your internal experience is available to you, it becomes easy to treat intention as the most accurate measure of your relational contribution. But your partner does not live inside your intention. They live with your behavior (Bradbury & Fincham, 1990; Baucom et al., 2011).

This does not mean intention is irrelevant. Intention matters because it can guide repair, reveal values, and create motivation for change. But intention does not erase impact. If a behavior repeats often enough, the relationship adapts to the behavior, not the explanation that follows it. The system is shaped by what happens consistently.

A person may intend to be emotionally available, but if they withdraw every time a difficult conversation begins, the relationship will organize around their withdrawal. A person may intend to be supportive, but if support appears only when it is convenient, the relationship will organize around unpredictability. A person may intend to be trustworthy, but if honesty arrives late, defensively, or only after pressure, the relationship will organize around caution. The system believes the pattern.

This is where potential becomes another common illusion. People often see potential in themselves and in others, and potential can be seductive because it allows the future to soften the present. It invites hope. It says, This could become something. This could improve. This person could grow. I could be different here. We could become better than what we are showing each other now.

Potential is not meaningless. It matters. Without potential, there is no development. But potential is not the same as readiness, and it is not the same as capacity. A grape has the potential to become wine, but potential alone does not make it wine. The transformation requires a process. It requires conditions, time, refinement, and change at the level of composition. Without that process, the potential remains real but unrealized.

Relationships often suffer because people fall in love with potential and then become resentful when it does not function like development.

They see what could be and begin relating to it as though it already exists. They imagine the patience, maturity, openness, consistency, or courage that might emerge under the right conditions. They confuse glimpses with structure. A moment of insight becomes proof of change. A sincere apology becomes evidence of readiness. A good week becomes a sign that the pattern has finally shifted. But development is not demonstrated by intensity in a moment. It is demonstrated by consistency over time.

A person's potential may be beautiful. It may even be accurate. But if it has not been developed, the relationship cannot rely on it. The relationship must function with what is available now, not only with what may become available later. This does not mean people should be judged harshly for being unfinished. Everyone is unfinished. It means that unfinished areas have consequences when they are brought into a system that requires dependability. A relationship can support growth. It cannot survive indefinitely on imagined growth.

This is especially important because the early stage of love often functions like an emotional campaign. It presents the most engaging version of what is possible. Attention is high. Energy is available. The desire to be understood and to understand the other person is active. Each person may be more patient, more curious, more responsive, and more generous than they are under ordinary conditions.

This is not necessarily deception. It is the effect of novelty, hope, attraction, and focus. In the beginning, people are often showing a real version of themselves, but it is a version supported by favorable conditions. They are not lying. They are not fully tested. The question is not whether the early version was real. The question is whether it is sustainable.

Every relationship eventually moves beyond the conditions that made the early version easy to maintain. The emotional campaign quiets. Novelty fades into familiarity. Other responsibilities return to their full weight. Stress exposes habits that attention once covered. The relationship begins to ask for a level of consistency that cannot be generated by excitement alone. This is when the product beneath the campaign becomes visible.

The relationship begins to discover what each person actually brings when the emotional environment is no longer ideal. How do they handle boredom? How do they handle unmet needs? How do they respond to correction? Do they repair after rupture, or do they wait for time to soften the issue? Do they take responsibility, or do they explain themselves so thoroughly that accountability disappears? Do they become curious when they do not understand, or do they assume the worst and respond to that assumption as though it is fact? These questions are not romantic in the conventional sense. They are more important than romance. They reveal whether the relationship has material it can build with.

People often do not know the answer to these questions until the relationship requires one. That is why the first significant disruption can feel so disorienting. It exposes the difference between what each person hoped they were building and what their patterns have actually created.

The disruption may be small. A concern is raised and the response is colder than expected. A boundary is expressed and treated as rejection. A need is named and met with defensiveness. A conflict begins and one person disappears into silence while the other grows increasingly urgent. A disappointment occurs and the apology feels more like an attempt to end the discomfort than a willingness to understand the harm. From the outside, the moment may not appear serious. Inside the relationship, something important has been revealed.

The first time the product fails is not always the first major crisis. It is the first moment when the relationship discovers that intention and function are not the same. It is the first time one person realizes that what they expected to receive in a difficult moment is not what the other person is currently able to provide. It is the first time the relationship encounters the limits of what has been developed.

This moment is often misread. One person may interpret it as evidence that the other does not care. The other may interpret the reaction as unfair, dramatic, or excessive. Both may focus on the event itself, debating whether the response was reasonable, whether the need was valid, whether the tone was appropriate, whether the timing was right. Those details may matter. But beneath them is a deeper question. What did this moment reveal about what we bring into difficulty?

That question begins to move the relationship toward clarity. It shifts attention from the surface of the conflict to the structure beneath it. It asks each person to examine not only what happened, but what happened automatically. What did I assume? What did I protect? What did I avoid? What did I demand? What did I repeat? What did I make the other person carry because I did not know how to carry it myself? This is the first honest look at oneself. It is also the look many people spend years avoiding.

The avoidance is understandable. Self-examination can feel like accusation when a person has only known responsibility as blame. To look at what you bring into love may feel, at first, like being asked to accept fault for everything that has happened. But this is not the purpose. The purpose is not to turn relational pain inward and call it growth. The purpose is to understand your participation accurately enough that change becomes possible. There is a difference between self-blame and self-responsibility.

Self-blame collapses complexity into personal failure. It says, This is all my fault. I ruin things. I am the problem. Self-responsibility is more precise. It says, I am part of what happens here. My patterns have effects. My reactions shape the system. My unexamined assumptions influence what I perceive and how I respond. I may not control the entire relationship, but I contribute to the conditions in which it develops. Self-blame leads to shame. Self-responsibility leads to agency.

Agency is essential because without it, a person remains dependent on finding someone who will somehow make their unexamined patterns irrelevant. That is a fragile way to love. It requires the other person to be endlessly patient, endlessly attuned, endlessly skilled at navigating responses they did not create. It turns compatibility into compensation. It asks the relationship to succeed by working around what has not been addressed. At some point, every relationship runs out of room for that. The unexamined self becomes expensive.

It costs clarity. It costs trust. It costs emotional safety. It costs the other person energy they may not have. It costs the relationship time because the same patterns have to be revisited repeatedly without being named accurately. It costs intimacy because intimacy cannot deepen where both people are busy managing what no one is willing to examine. This is why looking inward is not a private exercise separate from love. It is one of love's requirements.

What you do not understand about yourself will still participate in the relationship. Your lack of awareness does not protect the system from your patterns. It only makes those patterns harder to discuss. When you do not know why you react the way you do, the reaction is more likely to feel like truth. When you do not know what you are afraid of, your fear is more likely to become accusation. When you do not know what you need, you are more likely to punish the other person for not meeting it correctly. Unawareness does not keep things simple. It makes them harder to repair.

One of the clearest places this appears is in values. Most people believe they know their values in relationships. They say they want honesty, respect, loyalty, communication, commitment, emotional safety, and trust. These words are familiar enough to feel self-evident. They are also broad enough to hide enormous differences.

Two people can both value communication and mean entirely different things. One may define communication as frequent emotional sharing, while the other defines it as direct discussion when a problem needs to be solved. One may feel loved when feelings are named openly and often. The other may feel overwhelmed by that same level of expression and interpret it as pressure.

Two people can both value respect and still collide. One may define respect as honesty without avoidance. The other may define it as restraint, tone, and careful timing. One feel disrespected by silence. The other feels disrespected by confrontation. Both are using the same value to defend different behaviors.

Two people can both value commitment. For one, commitment means emotional reassurance, frequent contact, and visible prioritization. For the other, commitment means reliability, loyalty, and continuing to show up even when they are not verbally expressive. Neither definition is inherently wrong. But if they are not clarified, both people may feel unseen while believing they are offering exactly what the relationship requires. Values that remain undefined become sources of conflict (Ryan & Deci, 2000; Senge, 2006).

Not because values are unimportant, but because people often relate to the word rather than the behavior. They assume agreement at the level of language means alignment at the level of practice. It rarely does. The relationship does not function on abstract values. It functions on how those values are expressed, interpreted, and reinforced in daily life.

This is why a person must understand not only what they value, but how they operationalize what they value. What does honesty look like when the truth is uncomfortable? What does respect look like in conflict? What does loyalty require when family pressure, work pressure, or personal ambition pulls attention elsewhere? What does communication mean when one person needs time to process and the other needs immediate engagement? These questions reveal the invisible operating system beneath the relationship. Every person has one.

The operating system is the set of assumptions and rules that governs how love is understood. It tells you what certain behaviors mean. It tells you what closeness should feel like, what conflict signals, what silence implies, what commitment proves, what apology requires, and what safety should look like. It influences what you notice, what you ignore, what you expect, and what you fear. Most people do not recognize their operating system because it does not feel like an operating system. It feels like common sense.

This is where relationships become especially difficult. Each person assumes their way of interpreting love is obvious, reasonable, and shared. When the other person behaves differently, the difference is not experienced as difference. It is experienced as a violation of reality. If I mattered, they would respond more quickly. If they trusted me, they would not need so much reassurance. If they cared, they would know what I need without being told. If they respected me, they would not bring this up right now. If they loved me, this would not be so hard.

These statements may feel emotionally true. They may also reveal the assumptions that are running beneath the surface. The difficulty is that assumptions often appear most convincing when they are most unexamined. They arrive quickly, attach themselves to emotion, and begin directing behavior before the person has paused long enough to ask whether the interpretation is accurate. A relationship cannot become a learning system until the operating systems inside it become visible (Tversky & Kahneman, 1974; Kahneman, 2011).

This begins with humility. Not the performative humility of self-criticism, but the practical humility of recognizing that your first interpretation may not be the whole truth. The meaning you assign may have more history in it than evidence. The reaction that feels justified may be intensified by something older than the current moment. The expectation that feels obvious to you may be unfamiliar to the person you expect to meet it. This does not mean you distrust yourself. It means you become more precise with yourself.

Precision matters because relational patterns are often built through small misreadings that accumulate. One person interprets quietness as distance and responds with pressure. The other experiences pressure as criticism and responds with withdrawal. The withdrawal confirms the first person's fear of distance. The pressure confirms the second person's fear of being controlled. Neither is responding only to the other. Each is responding through an operating system that assigns meaning to behavior. The pattern feels personal. It is also structural.

Once this is understood, the question changes. Instead of asking only whether the other person is right for you, you begin asking what kind of system your patterns are likely to create with theirs. This is not less romantic. It is more honest. A relationship does not become strong because two people have appealing qualities in isolation. It becomes strong when the interaction between those qualities can function over time.

A person's sensitivity may become empathy in one system and hypervigilance in another. A person's independence may become steadiness in one system and emotional distance in another. A person's directness may become clarity in one system and harshness in another. A person's flexibility may become generosity in one system and self-erasure in another. Traits do not function alone. They function in interaction.

That is why what you bring into love cannot be evaluated only by how it appears in you. It must be understood by what it produces between you and another person. This is where the relationship becomes a mirror, though not always a flattering one. It reflects back the effects of patterns you may have only understood from the inside.

You may discover that what you call honesty lands as criticism because it is delivered without enough care. You may discover that what you call patience is actually avoidance because it delays necessary conversations until resentment has already formed. You may discover that what you call independence is a refusal to let anyone matter enough to inconvenience you. You may discover that what you call love is, at times, a desire to be chosen strongly enough that you no longer have to regulate your own fear. These discoveries can be uncomfortable, but they are not failures. They are data.

They reveal the difference between who you believe you are in love and how you actually function in love. That difference is one of the most important spaces for growth. Not because you must become someone else, but because your self-understanding must become accurate enough to support the kind of relationship you say you want. Accuracy is more useful than self-protection.

Self-protection often edits the story to preserve identity. It says, I am not the kind of person who does that. I only reacted because they made me. I would not be this way if they were different. There may be partial truth in those statements. Relationships do influence behavior. Some dynamics bring out parts of us that healthier systems would not reinforce. But if the pattern appears repeatedly across different relationships, different conflicts, or different seasons of life, it deserves attention. Repeated patterns are not accidents. They are invitations.

This does not mean every repeated relational difficulty belongs to you alone. Some patterns repeat because people choose similar partners, tolerate similar dynamics, or confuse familiar pain with connection. Some repeat because the person has not yet learned to recognize early signs of incompatibility, emotional unavailability, or misalignment. Some repeat because old wounds shape what feels compelling. In each case, the repeated pattern still offers information. Not about your worth. About your system.

This distinction protects the work from becoming moralistic. The goal is not to sort people into ready and unready, mature and immature, healthy and unhealthy. Human beings are more complicated than that. The goal is to understand readiness as a moving capacity, something that can be developed through awareness, practice, feedback, and repair. You are not condemned by what you bring into love. But you are responsible for learning what it does once it gets there.

That responsibility becomes more important as the relationship deepens. In the beginning, two people can often survive on attraction, attention, and shared hope. As the relationship grows, it begins requiring more: the ability to name needs without accusation, to hear discomfort without retaliation, to stay present without controlling the outcome, to admit impact without disappearing into shame, to negotiate difference without turning it into threat.

These are not abstract ideals. They are functional requirements. Without them, the relationship may still continue, but it will begin developing workarounds. One person will stop bringing up certain things because the reaction is too difficult. The other will stop sharing certain feelings because they never seem to land correctly. Both will begin managing the system instead of trusting it. Management is not intimacy.

A managed relationship can appear stable for a time. Conflict may be reduced. Routines may continue. The couple may function well enough from the outside. But underneath, the relationship becomes narrower. Less is said. Less is risked. Less is repaired. Each person learns the limits of what the system can hold and begins shaping themselves around those limits. This is often mistaken for maturity. Sometimes it is simply adaptation to underdevelopment.

A healthy relationship requires adaptation, but not all adaptation is healthy. Some adaptation expands the system. It helps two people understand each other more deeply, respond more wisely, and create new patterns. Other adaptation contracts the system. It teaches people to avoid the truth, mute their needs, soften their personalities, or accept instability as the cost of connection.

The difference lies in whether the adaptation leads to greater clarity and capacity or greater suppression and confusion.

What you bring into love will influence which direction adaptation takes. If you bring curiosity, the system has a better chance of expanding. If you bring defensiveness, the system contracts around protection. If you bring responsibility, repair becomes possible. If you bring avoidance, repair is delayed until damage accumulates. If you bring emotional regulation, conflict can become information. If you bring reactivity, conflict becomes threat. Again, this is not about perfection. It is about patterns strong enough to hold stress.

Every relationship will encounter stress. The question is not whether stress appears, but what it reveals. Stress will reveal whether the relationship is built on shared capacity or private coping. It will reveal whether communication is a value or only a preference when things are comfortable. It will reveal whether accountability exists beyond the moment of being confronted. It will reveal whether affection can survive inconvenience, whether commitment can survive disappointment, and whether both people can remain human to each other when neither feels at their best. Stress does not always create the problem. It exposes what the relationship has been relying on.

If the relationship has relied primarily on emotional momentum, stress will feel like the enemy of love. If it has built enough structure, stress becomes information the system can use. The difference is shaped, in part, by what each person brings into the moment.

This is why preparation for love cannot be reduced to finding the right partner. It also involves becoming more aware of the self that will participate in the relationship once that partner is found. Without that awareness, the search for love can become a cycle of external evaluation. Is this person right? Are they enough? Do they make me feel the way I want to feel? Can they give me what I have been missing? Those questions may be necessary, but they are incomplete.

The deeper question is: who do I become in the presence of another person's needs, limits, fears, differences, and imperfections? That question reveals readiness more accurately than longing does.

It is easy to imagine oneself loving well in ideal conditions. It is harder to love well when the other person is tired, distracted, disappointed, defensive, afraid, or not meeting an expectation. It is harder when the relationship asks for patience instead of intensity, repair instead of pride, and honesty instead of performance. It is harder when love requires not simply being chosen, but becoming trustworthy in the ordinary repetition of daily life.

This is where the business metaphor returns, not as a cold comparison, but as a useful discipline. In any serious enterprise, there is a difference between vision and execution. Vision matters because it gives direction. But vision without execution becomes fantasy. A person may have a beautiful idea of the relationship they want, but if their daily patterns do not support that idea, the relationship will not be built from the vision. It will be built from the execution.

You may want a relationship defined by trust, but if your behavior is inconsistent, the system will learn inconsistency. You may want a relationship defined by openness, but if you punish honesty with defensiveness, the system will learn caution. You may want a relationship defined by teamwork, but if you retreat into private coping whenever stress rises, the system will learn separation. You may want a relationship defined by peace, but if peace depends on avoiding every difficult conversation, the system will learn silence, not safety. The relationship you intend and the relationship you build are not always the same. That gap is where much of the work begins.

To close the gap, you have to observe what you actually do. Not what you believe about yourself. Not what you promised. Not what you meant. Not what you would do under better circumstances. What you actually do. How you respond. How you recover. How you ask. How you avoid. How you repair. How you handle the truth when it arrives from someone else's mouth.

This kind of observation requires courage because it removes the comfort of abstraction. It is one thing to say you value growth. It is another to notice that you resist feedback the moment it threatens your self-image. It is one thing to say you want a conscious relationship. It is another to notice that consciousness requires attention to parts of yourself you would rather leave unnamed. But this is also where dignity enters the process.

There is dignity in becoming someone who can see themselves clearly. There is dignity in no longer outsourcing every relational difficulty to fate, chemistry, timing, or the other person's limitations. There is dignity in recognizing that love is not only something you receive, but something your own patterns either strengthen or strain. The first honest look at yourself is not meant to diminish you. It is meant to bring you into the relationship as a more conscious participant.

That consciousness changes what you notice. You begin to hear your own tone before it hardens. You begin to recognize the story your mind adds to a moment before you treat it as fact. You begin to see the familiar sequence forming before you fully enter it. You begin to understand that your reaction may be understandable and still not useful. You begin to separate what you feel from what the relationship needs next. This is the beginning of relational maturity.

Not the absence of emotion, but the ability to remain responsible in the presence of emotion. Not the absence of old patterns, but the willingness to notice them before they run the system. Not the absence of fear, but the capacity to keep fear from becoming the architect of the relationship.

A person does not become ready for love by eliminating every wound, resolving every insecurity, or achieving some final state of self-mastery. That standard would make love impossible. Readiness begins when a person becomes willing to examine what they bring, understand its effects, and participate in changing the patterns that do not support the relationship they want to build. This willingness matters more than polish.

Polish can be misleading. People can present well. They can communicate beautifully when the stakes are low. They can speak the language of growth, healing, boundaries, and emotional intelligence while still becoming rigid, avoidant, or reactive when the relationship requires actual change. The language of maturity is not the same as maturity. The ability to describe a pattern is not the same as the ability to interrupt it. The relationship will eventually reveal the difference. It always does.

Because relationships are not sustained by self-concept. They are sustained by repeated behavior inside a shared system. What you bring will be tested by time, pressure, disappointment, routine, uncertainty, and the simple difficulty of living close to another human being. The purpose of seeing this is not to become afraid of love. It is to enter love with enough respect for its demands that you stop expecting feeling to carry what only awareness can carry. You do not need to arrive perfect. But you do need to arrive awake.

Awake to your assumptions. Awake to your patterns. Awake to the difference between desire and capacity. Awake to the ways potential must be developed before it can be relied upon. Awake to the fact that your inner life does not remain private once it begins shaping another person's experience. This is where the illusion of love begins to give way to the system of love.

Chapter 1 challenged the belief that love works simply because it feels right. This chapter adds the next truth: even when the feeling is real, the relationship will still have to work with what each person brings into it. Love is not built by feeling alone, and it is not built by finding alone. It is built through the interaction of two people whose histories, habits, fears, values, and capacities become part of the same living structure. The question, then, is not only whether you have found love. The question is what love finds when it finds you.

Does it find someone willing to observe themselves? Someone willing to learn the effect of their patterns? Someone willing to define their values beyond attractive language? Someone willing to close the gap between intention and behavior? Someone willing to develop potential into capacity? These questions are not asked to create judgment. They are asked to create honesty.

Because the relationship will eventually ask them, whether you ask them first or not. It will ask them in conflict, in silence, in disappointment, in repair, in the moments where the early story is no longer enough. It will ask them when stress enters, when assumptions collide, when the emotional campaign fades, and when the system beneath the feeling begins to show itself. What you bring into those moments will shape what happens next. And that is why the relationship begins before the relationship begins. By the time love arrives, you are already carrying the material from which part of it will be built.

PART II
THE SYSTEM

Once the illusion begins to weaken, the relationship becomes visible in a different way.

It is no longer enough to ask whether the feeling is real, whether the connection is strong, or whether two people want the same general future. Those questions still matter, but they no longer explain enough. A relationship can contain real feeling, genuine connection, sincere desire, and shared intention, yet still become unstable because the system underneath it has never been understood. This is where Part II begins.

A relationship is not only an emotional bond between two people. It is a living pattern of interaction. It is shaped by what each person brings into it, but it becomes something more than either individual alone. Over time, the relationship develops its own rhythm, its own expectations, its own repeated sequences, its own forms of tension and repair. Certain conversations become predictable. Certain reactions become familiar. Certain issues return with different details but the same emotional structure. At some point, the relationship is no longer simply made of what each person feels. It is made of what repeatedly happens between them. That is the system.

Most people do not see the system at first. They see the argument, the silence, the disappointment, the tone, the delayed response, the unmet need, the moment that seemed to change the room. They see the visible disruption and try to fix it directly. But the visible disruption is rarely the whole problem. It is usually the place where the deeper pattern has become noticeable. Part II shifts the focus from the event to the structure beneath it.

Chapter 3, "Systems Thinking in Love," introduces the central lens of the book. It asks the reader to stop treating relational problems as isolated incidents and begin seeing them as expressions of a larger pattern. The argument is not only the argument. The withdrawal is not only the withdrawal. The overreaction is not only the overreaction. Each moment belongs to a sequence, and the sequence is often more important than the event itself.

Chapter 4, "Personal Mastery," moves from the system to the self-inside the system. Once the pattern becomes visible, the next question is unavoidable: what do you do with yourself when the system becomes stressful? Personal mastery is not control, suppression, or emotional performance. It is the ability to observe your own reaction, understand what is being activated, and choose a response that does not simply reinforce the pattern you say you want to change.

Chapter 5, "Mental Models," examines the invisible rules and assumptions that shape how people interpret love. No one reacts to a relationship from pure reality. Each person reacts through a lens built from memory, belief, family, culture, fear, and prior experience. Until those lenses are examined, two people may continue arguing not only about what happened, but about what they believe it means.

The purpose of this section is not to make love mechanical. It is to make love understandable. A system is not the opposite of intimacy. It is the structure through which intimacy either becomes sustainable or begins to break down. When the system remains invisible, people are left reacting to outcomes they do not understand. When the system becomes visible, the relationship becomes something that can be observed, questioned, and changed. That is where the work becomes different. Not easier. Different.

CHAPTER THREE

SYSTEMS THINKING IN LOVE

Why the Problem Is Never Just the Problem

There is a kind of argument that reveals more than it appears to reveal.

It does not always begin dramatically. In fact, it may begin with something small enough that neither person would have predicted where it was headed. A question is asked with a certain tone. A response arrives a little too quickly or a little too late. One person makes a comment that seems ordinary to them and loaded to the other. A small correction is heard as criticism. A request is heard as pressure. A pause is heard as distance. Within minutes, the room changes.

The conversation is no longer about the thing that started it. Both people can sense this, even if neither can fully explain it. The subject is still there on the surface, but it no longer contains the emotional force of the moment. Something else has entered. The intensity feels larger than the issue. The reaction seems disproportionate. The history of the relationship has arrived without being invited.

Afterward, when the argument has ended or exhausted itself, both people may try to make sense of what happened. They review the sequence. One says, "I only asked a question." The other says, "It was the way you asked it." One says, "You overreacted." The other says, "You always do this." The conversation becomes an autopsy of the event, but the event alone cannot explain the size of what occurred. That is because the argument did not exist by itself. It belonged to a system.

Most people are trained to understand relationships through events. Something happens, and attention goes to that happening. The missed call, the forgotten errand, the comment at dinner, the silence in the car, the conversation that became tense without warning. Because the event is visible, it becomes the presumed source of the problem. If the event can be explained, then perhaps the problem can be solved. But in relationships, the visible event is often only the latest expression of an invisible pattern. The problem is rarely just the problem.

This is one of the first and most important principles of systems thinking in love. A relationship is not a series of disconnected moments. It is an organized pattern of interaction that develops over time. Each moment affects the next. Each reaction teaches the system something. Each unresolved injury, each avoided conversation, each successful repair, each repeated disappointment, and each familiar defense becomes part of the structure through which the relationship operates (von Bertalanffy, 1968; Watzlawick et al., 1967; Meadows, 2008).

A system is not simply a collection of parts. It is the way those parts interact. In a relationship, the parts are not only two individuals. They include each person's history, assumptions, fears, emotional habits, coping strategies, expectations, values, needs, interpretations, and learned responses. They include what is said and what is withheld. They include timing, tone, body language, memory, repetition, and meaning. They include all the small ways two people influence each other without realizing they are doing it. Over time, these elements begin to organize themselves. That organization becomes the relationship.

This is why two relationships with similar problems can function very differently. One couple can disagree often and remain emotionally safe because disagreement has been integrated into a system of honesty, repair, humor, and mutual respect. Another couple can rarely argue and still feel fragile because silence has become a way of avoiding what neither person knows how to address. The event is not enough to tell us what is happening. A disagreement is not always a sign of instability. Calm is not always a sign of health. The meaning of an event depends on the system around it.

If a person says, "I need space," the statement can mean very different things in different systems. In one relationship, it may mean, "I am overwhelmed, and I need time so I can return to this conversation more thoughtfully." In another, it may mean, "I am leaving this unresolved because I do not know how to stay engaged." In one system, space is a form of regulation. In another, it is a form of withdrawal. The words are the same. The pattern gives them meaning.

This is why relational problems so often feel confusing. People argue about the words because the words are easier to identify than the system that gives them force. They debate whether the statement was fair, whether the tone was justified, whether the timing was appropriate. Those details may matter, but they are not the whole picture. The deeper question is what the moment activated inside the established pattern. A systems view asks different questions. Not only, "What happened?" but, "What keeps happening?" (Senge, 2006; Meadows, 2008)

Not only, "Who started it?" but, "What sequence are we both participating in?"

Not only, "Why did this become so intense?" but, "What history did this moment carry?"

Not only, "How do we stop this argument?" but, "What structure keeps producing this kind of argument?"

These questions do not remove accountability. They make accountability more precise. They move the relationship away from the illusion that the whole problem can be located in a single person, a single sentence, or a single emotional reaction. They ask both people to look at the pattern that made the moment more likely. This is difficult because blame is much easier than pattern recognition.

Blame offers the relief of simplicity. It tells the mind where to place the pain. If the problem is you, then I can be innocent. If the problem is me, then perhaps I can punish myself into change. Either way, blame reduces complexity into a single point of responsibility. It creates an answer quickly, and quick answers are emotionally seductive when a relationship feels unstable. But blame rarely changes the system.

It may identify a behavior that matters. It may call attention to a real harm. It may name something that cannot be ignored. But when blame becomes the primary lens, it narrows the field of vision. One person becomes the problem, and the interaction disappears. The system remains intact because the relationship is now focused on defending, accusing, explaining, or withdrawing rather than observing what repeatedly happens between the two people. This is why many couples can have the same argument for years. The topic changes. The pattern does not.

One month the argument is about money. Another month it is about time. Another month it is about family, intimacy, parenting, work, or a decision that should have been simple. The surface issue shifts, which creates the illusion that the couple is dealing with different problems. But underneath, the same sequence may be repeating. One person feels unseen and becomes urgent. The other feels attacked and becomes defensive. The urgency increases. The defensiveness hardens. The conversation collapses into familiar positions. The couple thinks they are arguing about money, time, family, or priorities. The system is arguing about safety, influence, recognition, and control.

Once the system is active, the specific issue becomes less important than the pattern it triggers. This does not mean the issue is irrelevant. Money matters.

Time matters. Family matters. Intimacy matters. Decisions matter. But the issue is often the doorway through which the system enters. If the system is organized around defensiveness and pursuit, almost any important topic can become the stage on which that pattern performs.

This is where systems thinking begins to change the emotional experience of the relationship. It does not ask people to stop caring about the moment. It asks them to understand that the moment is part of a larger structure. The delayed response is not only a delayed response if delayed responses have repeatedly been experienced as disregard. The sharp tone is not only a sharp tone if tone has become the early signal that criticism is coming. The forgotten task is not only a forgotten task if forgotten tasks have come to represent unreliability. The event may be small. The pattern may not be.

When people do not see this, they often accuse each other of overreacting. The accusation may seem reasonable from an event-based perspective. If the event is small, then a strong reaction appears excessive. But from a systems perspective, the reaction may be responding not only to the event but to what the event represents inside the pattern.

This does not mean every reaction is justified. A strong emotional response may still be disproportionate, damaging, or poorly regulated. But if the goal is understanding rather than judgment, the question becomes more useful: what did this small moment connect to? What did it confirm, threaten, or reopen? Why did this particular event carry more meaning than it seemed to deserve? The answers usually live in repetition.

Repetition is the language of systems. A single moment may be accidental. A repeated moment becomes information. A partner being distracted once may mean very little. A partner being unavailable every time a vulnerable topic is raised means something more. A person becoming defensive once may reflect stress or fatigue. A person becoming defensive every time impact is discussed becomes a pattern the relationship must address. The system is built in repetition because repetition teaches expectation. Expectation then shapes perception (Skinner, 1953; Baer et al., 1968).

This is why patterns become self-reinforcing. Once a person expects dismissal, they listen for it. Once they expect criticism, they brace for it. Once they expect withdrawal, they monitor for distance. These expectations are not always conscious, but they influence the way each person enters the interaction. The body prepares before the conversation has unfolded. The voice tightens. The timing changes. The first sentence is chosen with the old outcome already in mind. The system begins before the argument does.

By the time the issue is spoken aloud, both people may already be responding to a history that has not been named. This is why conversations can feel tense before anything difficult has actually been said. The pattern is present in the anticipation. One person approaches carefully because they expect defensiveness. The other senses the carefulness and experiences it as judgment. One waits too long to speak and then speaks with accumulated frustration. The other hears the frustration and feels ambushed. Each response makes sense from the inside. Together, they recreate the system. No one set out to do it. Both helped make it happen.

This is one of the hardest truths of systems thinking. A relationship can produce outcomes neither person consciously wants. Two people can both want closeness and still create distance. They can both want peace and still reinforce conflict. They can both want honesty and still build a system where the truth feels unsafe. They can both want partnership and still operate as two defended individuals trying to survive the same conversation. Good intentions do not automatically produce a healthy system. The system responds to behavior.

This is where behavioral science becomes useful, not as a cold way of analyzing love, but as a way of understanding how patterns are strengthened. Within any relationship, behaviors are shaped by what follows them. If a behavior reduces discomfort, even temporarily, it becomes more likely to be repeated. If withdrawal ends the argument, withdrawal is reinforced. If escalation finally gets a response, escalation is reinforced. If defensiveness prevents shame, defensiveness is reinforced. If appeasement restores temporary peace, appeasement is reinforced. The relationship begins training both people (Skinner, 1953; Baer et al., 1968).

Applied behavior analysis adds discipline to this question by asking what a behavior does in context. The issue is not only what the behavior looks like, but what happens before it, what happens after it, and what consequence makes it more likely to return. In a relationship, the consequence may be relief from shame, avoidance of conflict, temporary reassurance, restored closeness, or escape from overwhelm. This is why a response can be damaging and still become reinforced. It works in the moment, even if it weakens the system over time (Skinner, 1953; Baer et al., 1968).

Most couples do not realize this is happening. They think they are simply reacting. But every reaction teaches the system something about what works, at least in the short term. The problem is that what works in the short term may damage the relationship over time.

Avoiding a difficult conversation may reduce tension tonight, but it teaches the system that discomfort is managed through silence. Pressuring a partner may produce engagement in the moment, but it teaches the system that connection must be forced. Explaining defensively may protect self-image, but it teaches the system that impact will be debated before it is understood. Apologizing quickly may end the conflict, but it teaches the system that repair can be performed without transformation. The system learns from outcomes, not intentions.

A couple may say they value communication, but if honesty is repeatedly met with punishment, the system will learn caution. They may say they value emotional safety, but if vulnerability is repeatedly met with correction, the system will learn guardedness. They may say they value partnership, but if stress is repeatedly handled in isolation, the system will learn separation. What is reinforced becomes the relationship (Skinner, 1953; Wolf, 1978).

This is why relationship change is so difficult. People often try to change the system through statements of intention. They say, "I will do better." "I do not want us to keep doing this." "I know this has to change." These statements may be sincere, and sincerity matters. But the system does not reorganize around sincerity alone. It reorganizes around repeated behavior that is different enough and consistent enough to create a new pattern. A system has momentum.

That momentum can make old patterns feel inevitable. The relationship seems to move in the same direction even when both people are trying to avoid it. A conversation begins with restraint and still ends in the familiar place. One person promises not to withdraw and still shuts down when overwhelmed. The other promises not to escalate and still becomes urgent when they feel ignored. Both may leave the conversation feeling defeated, not only by each other, but by the relationship itself. This is the point where the system feels stronger than the individuals.

It is not actually stronger in some mystical sense. It is simply better practiced. The pattern has been repeated more often than the alternative. The nervous system recognizes the old sequence. The mind knows its role. The body prepares for the familiar outcome. The relationship moves through the old pathway because that pathway has been reinforced. New patterns feel awkward because they are not yet practiced (Stokes & Baer, 1977; Bandura, 1977).

A person trying to respond differently may feel unnatural at first. The pause feels strange. The softer tone feels vulnerable. The honest statement feels risky. The refusal to defend feels exposed. The decision to stay present instead of withdrawing may feel almost physically uncomfortable. This discomfort does not mean the new response is wrong. It means the system has not yet learned it. The old pattern will often resist the new one.

If one person changes their response, the other may not trust it immediately. This is important. A system that has been built through repetition does not transform because of one different moment. The person who has experienced years of defensiveness may not relax after one nondefensive response. The person who has experienced repeated withdrawal may not feel safe after one moment of staying. The person who has experienced unreliable repair may not trust one apology, no matter how sincere. Systems change through consistency.

This requires patience that many people underestimate. Not patience as passive waiting, but patience as sustained behavioral evidence. A new pattern has to be repeated long enough for the relationship to learn that it can rely on something different. Trust is not restored by the announcement of change. It is restored when the system repeatedly encounters change and survives it. This is why systems thinking is both sobering and hopeful.

It is sobering because it reveals that one good conversation is usually not enough. One apology is not enough. One insight is not enough. One weekend of closeness is not enough to undo a pattern that has been reinforced over months or years. A system does not become unstable overnight, and it does not become stable again through emotional intensity alone. But systems thinking is hopeful because it shows that repeated patterns can be changed by repeated differences.

The relationship is not fixed simply because it feels familiar. What has been built can be rebuilt. What has been reinforced can be interrupted. What has become predictable can become more flexible. But the work has to happen at the level of the system, not merely at the level of isolated events.

To work at the level of the system, both people must begin seeing their interactions differently. They must learn to notice sequences rather than only moments. They must become curious about what happens before the conflict becomes obvious. They must ask what each response makes more likely. They must recognize the places where the relationship rewards what harms it and neglects what could strengthen it.

This is also where the behavioral concept of social validity matters. A relational change is not meaningful simply because it looks better from the outside or because it satisfies one person's preferred standard. It must matter to the people living inside the relationship. The goals must be worth pursuing, the practices must be acceptable enough to sustain, and the outcomes must improve the lived quality of the system. In that sense, repair is not only technically effective; it must also be humanly meaningful (Wolf, 1978; Kazdin, 1977).

This kind of awareness is not easy because it interferes with self-protection. When hurt, most people want validation before perspective. They want the other person to admit fault, recognize impact, and repair the damage. These needs are not wrong. But if the relationship never moves beyond them, the system remains unseen. Each person stays focused on their own injury, and the larger pattern continues to reproduce the conditions for future injury. Systems thinking does not ask people to abandon their pain. It asks them to place their pain inside a larger truth.

The pain is real. The behavior matters. The impact should be understood. But the question must eventually widen. What keeps producing this pain? What sequence keeps making this behavior more likely? What does each person do, avoid, assume, or reinforce that keeps the pattern alive? This widening is the beginning of relational intelligence.

It allows two people to stop treating every painful moment as a fresh emergency and begin recognizing the deeper architecture that keeps generating emergencies. It changes the conversation from accusation to investigation. Not in a detached, clinical way, but in a mature way. The goal is no longer to win the moment. The goal is to understand the system well enough to change the future. This is where accountability becomes more powerful, not less.

In a blame-based relationship, accountability often becomes a weapon. One person uses it to demand admission, the other experiences it as attack, and the conversation turns into a negotiation over fault. In a systems-aware relationship, accountability becomes more exact. Each person is asked to own their behavior, their impact, and their contribution to the pattern. The point is not to equalize responsibility artificially. Some behaviors carry more harm than others. Some patterns are more dangerous, more one-sided, or more damaging. Systems thinking does not flatten those realities. What it does is prevent the relationship from confusing explanation with excuse.

To understand a pattern is not to justify every behavior within it. It is possible to say, "This is how the system developed," and also say, "This behavior is not acceptable." It is possible to recognize that withdrawal was learned as self-protection and still require engagement. It is possible to understand that escalation comes from fear and still insist that fear cannot be expressed through aggression. It is possible to see the system and still set boundaries within it. In fact, seeing the system often makes boundaries clearer.

When people view problems only as events, they may argue endlessly about whether a particular moment was serious enough to justify a response. When they see the system, they can recognize the cumulative effect. A single dismissive comment may be survivable. A pattern of dismissal reshapes the emotional climate. A single broken promise may be repairable. A pattern of broken promises reorganizes the relationship around doubt. A single silence may be understandable. A pattern of silence teaches the relationship that vulnerability will be met with absence. The system reveals what the event can hide.

This matters especially when the relationship contains harm. Systems thinking should never be used to pressure someone to remain in a damaging or unsafe situation. Some systems are not merely underdeveloped; they are destructive. Some patterns do not require better communication; they require protection, distance, intervention, or exit. Understanding a system does not obligate anyone to preserve it. Clarity may reveal what can be repaired, but it may also reveal what cannot continue. A mature systems view includes that possibility.

It does not romanticize endurance. It does not treat every relationship as a project worth saving. It asks whether the system is capable of learning, whether both people are willing to observe and change, and whether the relationship is safe enough for the work it requires. Without those conditions, systems language can become another way to delay necessary decisions. But when both people are willing, systems thinking becomes one of the most useful shifts a relationship can make.

It allows a couple to see that their recurring conflicts are not random failures of character. They are structured interactions. It allows them to identify where the sequence begins, how it accelerates, and what each person does that keeps it alive. It allows them to change the question from "What is wrong with us?" to "What are we repeatedly creating, and how do we create something different?" That question changes the emotional atmosphere.

Instead of standing across from each other as opponents, two people can begin standing beside each other as observers of the pattern. The pattern becomes the shared problem. Not the only problem, and not a way of avoiding individual responsibility, but the thing they are trying to understand together. This shift can soften defensiveness because the conversation is no longer organized entirely around accusation. It can also strengthen accountability because each person can see where their own behavior enters the sequence.

A relationship begins to mature when both people can say, in some form, "Here is what happens to me in this pattern, and here is what I do that helps keep it going." That sentence requires courage.

It requires a person to be honest without collapsing into shame. It requires them to acknowledge impact without making themselves the entire problem. It requires them to look at their partner's behavior with enough clarity to name what hurts, and enough humility to recognize their own participation. This is not easy work. It is not always clean. It often begins clumsily, with defensiveness still present and old reactions still close to the surface. But even clumsy awareness changes the system more than polished blame.

Once a couple can observe the pattern, they can begin looking for leverage points. A leverage point is a place in the sequence where a small but consistent change can alter what happens next. In relationships, leverage points often appear earlier than people expect. They may occur before the argument begins; in the moment a person assigns meaning to a tone. They may occur in the first response to a concern. They may occur when one person feels the urge to withdraw, defend, criticize, appease, or pursue. The earlier the pattern is interrupted, the more room the relationship has to move differently. A pause can become a leverage point. A clarifying question can become a leverage point. A softer beginning can become a leverage point. A direct request can become a leverage point. An honest admission of fear can become a leverage point. A decision to return to the conversation after taking space can become a leverage point (Meadows, 2008; Forrester, 1968).

None of these changes is dramatic by itself. But systems are often changed through repeated small differences, not grand emotional declarations. A relationship becomes different when enough moments become different. The old pathway weakens because it is no longer followed every time. The new pathway strengthens because it is practiced often enough to become available under stress. This is how a relationship learns.

It does not learn because both people understand the concept intellectually. It learns because the pattern of interaction changes in lived experience. The system receives different inputs and begins producing different outputs. A concern raised with less accusation is met with less defensiveness. A defensive impulse is interrupted before it becomes an argument. A need is named directly instead of expressed through resentment. A withdrawal is followed by a return instead of disappearance. A conflict ends not with exhaustion, but with repair. Each moment teaches the system what is now possible.

This is why the idea of a learning relationship depends first on systems thinking. A relationship cannot learn from what it cannot see. If every problem is treated as a separate event, the couple remains trapped in reaction. If every conflict is reduced to fault, the system remains hidden. If every emotional shift is interpreted as proof that something is wrong, the relationship never develops the capacity to understand its own movement. Systems thinking gives the relationship a way to see itself.

That seeing is not abstract. It is practical. It changes what people notice in real time. A person begins to recognize, "This is where I usually defend." Another begins to notice, "This is where I usually push harder." Someone realizes, "This silence is not neutral; it has a history in our relationship." Someone else realizes, "My urgency may be making the very thing I fear more likely." These recognitions do not solve the pattern immediately, but they create space inside it. Space is where change begins.

Without space, the pattern runs automatically. The reaction becomes the behavior. The behavior becomes the next trigger. The loop continues. With space, even a small amount, a person can choose something that does not belong to the old sequence. They can ask instead of accuse. They can name instead of perform. They can pause instead of vanish. They can listen for impact instead of preparing a defense. The system begins to loosen.

The first time this happens, it may feel fragile. The old pattern may still be close. Both people may feel unsure of the new response. They may not trust it yet. That is normal. A new system is not built from one successful moment. It is built from the willingness to keep returning to the new pattern until it becomes more reliable than the old one.

This is why systems thinking must be paired with patience. Not passive patience, and not tolerance of harm, but developmental patience. The patience to understand that repeated behavior built the current system and repeated behavior will be required to change it. The patience to see early attempts not as final proof, but as practice. The patience to measure change not only by whether conflict disappears, but by whether the relationship recovers differently, understands itself sooner, and returns to connection with more honesty. The goal is not to create a relationship without conflict.

A conflict-free relationship may be peaceful, or it may be silent. It may be stable, or it may be avoidant. The absence of conflict does not prove the presence of health. The more useful goal is a relationship that can use conflict as information without being consumed by it. A relationship that can identify the pattern, name the impact, repair the rupture, and adjust the behavior that made the rupture more likely. That is a different kind of strength.

It is not the strength of never being tested. It is the strength of becoming more capable after being tested. It is the strength of a system that can observe itself, learn from itself, and reorganize around what it discovers. This is where love becomes less passive.

If love is understood only as a feeling, then relational difficulty becomes a threat to the feeling. If love is understood as a system, then difficulty becomes information about how the system is functioning. The feeling still matters. It may ache, shift, intensify, quiet, or return in different forms. But the relationship is no longer dependent on feeling alone to explain what is happening. It has a way to understand its own structure. That understanding changes what people are responsible for.

Each person is still responsible for their own behavior. That does not disappear. But they are also responsible for becoming aware of the pattern their behavior participates in. A person cannot control the entire system by themselves, but they can control whether they continue feeding the sequence in the same way. They can control whether they remain unconscious inside the loop or begin looking for the moment where they can choose differently. This brings the work of systems thinking to an uncomfortable but necessary point. Once you can see the system, you have to see yourself inside it.

It is tempting to use systems thinking to analyze the relationship from a distance, as though the system is something outside of you. But you are not outside of it. Your tone is part of it. Your timing is part of it. Your silence is part of it. Your assumptions are part of it. Your fear, your defensiveness, your avoidance, your urgency, your repair, your willingness to return—all of it enters the system and changes what happens next. This is not a reason for shame. It is a reason for responsibility.

The system may be larger than either individual, but every system has points of entry. In a relationship, the most immediate point of entry is always the self. Not because you are the whole problem, but because you are the part of the system you can access most directly. You may not be able to make another person listen, soften, repair, or change. But you can begin observing what happens in you when the system becomes stressful. You can learn how your own reactions contribute to the pattern. You can develop the capacity to remain present when the old sequence tries to take over. Systems thinking shows the pattern. Personal mastery asks what you will do once you see yourself in it. That is the next step.

CHAPTER FOUR

PERSONAL MASTERY

The One Thing You Cannot Avoid

Once a relationship is seen as a system, it becomes tempting to study the pattern from a distance.

The sequence becomes visible. One person reaches; the other withdraws. One criticizes; the other defends. One avoids; the other intensifies. The same emotional structure returns through different topics, and what once felt confusing begins to make a certain kind of sense. The relationship is no longer a series of isolated incidents. It is a living pattern, built through repetition, reinforced by response, and carried forward by what each person continues to do. This realization is useful, but it is also incomplete. Because once you see the system, you eventually have to see yourself inside it.

That is the part many people resist. It is easier to identify the pattern than to recognize the role you play in maintaining it. It is easier to say, "This is what happens between us," than to say, "This is what happens in me when the pattern begins." It is easier to analyze the relationship than to observe the version of yourself that enters the relationship when stress, fear, disappointment, or uncertainty appear. Systems thinking gives you the map. Personal mastery asks whether you can govern yourself while standing inside the territory.

This is not the kind of mastery that implies dominance, perfection, or emotional control in the rigid sense. It is not a performance of calmness. It is not the ability to appear unaffected when something hurts. It is not the suppression of feeling in order to seem mature. Personal mastery is something more difficult and more honest. It is the capacity to observe yourself in real time, especially when you are activated, and to choose a response that is not merely a repetition of your oldest pattern. It begins with a truth that sounds simple until it is tested. You brought yourself into this (Senge, 2006; Gross, 1998; Hayes et al., 2006).

Acceptance and Commitment Therapy offer a useful language for this kind of mastery because ACT does not define health as the absence of painful thoughts or feelings. It emphasizes psychological flexibility: the capacity to remain in contact with the present moment and act in the service of chosen values, even when discomfort is present. In relationship terms, this means the goal is not to stop feeling fear, shame, anger, longing, or uncertainty. The goal is to keep those feelings from automatically deciding how love will behave (Hayes et al., 2006; Hayes et al., 2012; Daks & Rogge, 2020).

Not just your affection, your hopes, your loyalty, your intentions, or your desire to love well. You brought your nervous system. You brought your interpretations. You brought your history. You brought your automatic reactions. You brought your fear of abandonment, your discomfort with conflict, your habit of withdrawing, your urgency to be understood, your instinct to defend, your tendency to overexplain, your impulse to disappear, your need to control the emotional temperature of the room. You brought the parts of yourself you are proud of. You also brought the parts that become most visible when love stops feeling easy.

This does not mean you are the problem. It means you are part of the system. There is a difference. To say that you are the problem collapses complexity into blame. To say that you are part of the system gives you a point of entry. It allows you to ask not only what the relationship is doing to you, but what you are doing inside the relationship.

That question is uncomfortable because it removes the innocence of pure reaction. It does not deny that you may be hurt. It does not deny that the other person may have behaved poorly, failed to listen, avoided responsibility, or contributed heavily to the pattern. Personal mastery does not ask you to absorb all responsibility or excuse what damages you. It asks you to become accurate about your own participation. Accuracy matters because every relationship is shaped, in part, by what people do when they feel threatened.

Most people know who they would like to be in love. They would like to be patient, honest, generous, emotionally steady, clear, forgiving, and brave enough to remain open when the relationship becomes difficult. They may genuinely believe these qualities describe them, and in many circumstances, they may. When conditions are favorable, when needs are met, when communication is warm, when uncertainty is low, it is not difficult to recognize the version of yourself you prefer. But relationships are not tested most deeply by the conditions that support your preferred self. They are tested by the conditions that call forward your practiced self.

The practiced self is the one that appears before reflection has fully arrived. It is the self that reacts from familiarity. It is the one that knows how to protect, pursue, retreat, argue, appease, numb, rationalize, charm, criticize, or shut down. It is not always the wisest self, but it is often the fastest. It has been rehearsed through years of experience. It knows what to do before you have decided what kind of person you want to be in the moment.

This is why people can surprise themselves in conflict. They hear their own voice harden. They watch themselves say the thing they promised they would not say. They feel the impulse to withdraw even while knowing withdrawal will wound the other person. They become defensive even when they can understand, somewhere beneath the reaction, that defensiveness will not help. They demand reassurance in a way that makes connection less likely. They stay silent when honesty is required. They try to end the discomfort instead of understanding what created it. Afterward, when the intensity has passed, they may feel confused by their own behavior. That was not what I meant. That is not who I want to be. I do not know why I reacted that way.

These statements may be sincere. They may also be true. But sincerity after the fact does not change the pattern unless it becomes awareness during the fact. A relationship is not shaped only by what you regret later. It is shaped by what you repeat when the moment is active. This is where personal mastery begins.

Not in the apology, though apology may be necessary. Not in the explanation, though explanation may help. It begins in the capacity to notice the reaction while it is forming, before it becomes the next piece of the pattern. This is harder than it sounds because reactions often feel like truth.

When you feel rejected, the rejection seems real. When you feel criticized, the criticism seems obvious. When you feel controlled, abandoned, dismissed, unseen, or disrespected, the emotional experience arrives with its own certainty. The body responds before the mind has finished gathering evidence. The heart rate shifts. The voice changes. Muscles tighten. Attention narrows. The other person's words are filtered through threat, and the relationship becomes smaller than it is.

In that state, the mind does not ask, "What is the most accurate interpretation of this moment?" It asks, "How do I protect myself?"

Protection is not always irrational. Some relationships do require protection. Some behaviors are unsafe, cruel, manipulative, or damaging.

Personal mastery should never be confused with tolerating harm or becoming endlessly patient with irresponsibility. There are moments when the wisest response is distance, boundary, or exit.

But many relational patterns are not built from clear danger. They are built from perceived threat. They are built from old meanings attached to present events. A partner's silence becomes abandonment. A request becomes criticism. A difference becomes rejection. A boundary becomes punishment. A concern becomes proof of failure. The mind assigns meaning quickly, and the body begins defending against the meaning as if it were fact. This is how the reaction you did not choose becomes the behavior you now have to answer for.

A reaction can be understandable and still be unhelpful. It can have a history and still create damage. It can protect you from discomfort in the moment and still weaken the relationship over time. This is one of the more difficult truths of personal mastery: the origin of a reaction does not determine its usefulness (Hayes et al., 2006; Daks & Rogge, 2020).

You may have learned to withdraw because, at some point, silence was safer than speaking. You may have learned to become urgent because being calm meant being ignored. You may have learned to control because unpredictability once carried real consequences. You may have learned to please because disagreement threatened connection. These responses may have been intelligent adaptations to earlier environments. But a response that once protected you can later imprison you.

In a relationship, old protections often become new constraints. They limit the range of what is possible. Withdrawal prevents repair. Urgency prevents listening. Control prevents trust. Pleasing prevents honesty. Defensiveness prevents accountability. Each response may reduce immediate discomfort, but it also teaches the relationship what it can expect from you under stress. The system learns your practiced self. Personal mastery is the work of becoming less governed by that self.

This does not happen through force. Many people hear the word mastery and imagine discipline in its harshest form: clamping down on emotion, controlling expression, refusing vulnerability, never raising one's voice, never needing reassurance, never being affected by what another person does. But that kind of control is not mastery. It is management. Sometimes it is even avoidance dressed as maturity. Control tries to dominate emotion. Regulation tries to understand and guide it (Gross, 1998; Gross & John, 2003; Bloch et al., 2014).

The difference matters. Control says, "I should not feel this." Regulation says, "I am feeling this, and I need to understand what it is asking of me before

I act." Control treats emotion as an enemy that must be contained. Regulation treats emotion as information that must be interpreted carefully. Control often creates pressure beneath the surface. Regulation creates space. Space is the essential ingredient.

Without space, the reaction becomes the behavior. The feeling becomes the sentence. The assumption becomes the accusation. The fear becomes the demand. The discomfort becomes the withdrawal. There is no room for choice because the old pattern moves too quickly. With space, even a small amount, something different becomes possible.

You can notice that you are angry before you weaponize the anger. You can notice that you feel rejected before you accuse the other person of not caring. You can notice the urge to disappear before you leave the conversation emotionally empty. You can notice the thought that says, "They should already know," before you punish them for not knowing. You can notice that your body is preparing for a fight that the present moment may not require. This does not make the feeling disappear. It gives you a chance to decide what the feeling means and what the relationship needs next.

Most people underestimate how much relational change depends on this moment. They look for change in major conversations, dramatic apologies, renewed commitments, or decisive breakthroughs. Those moments can matter, but much of the relationship is shaped in smaller spaces: the pause before the defensive reply, the breath before the accusation, the decision to ask rather than assume, the willingness to say, "I am starting to react, and I need a moment to understand what is happening in me." These are not small acts. They are structural interventions. A system changes when enough moments change. Personal mastery is how those moments become available.

This is the point where ABA and ACT meet in a particularly useful way. ABA helps identify what maintains the pattern: the antecedents, behaviors, consequences, and short-term reinforcers that keep the loop alive. ACT helps the person act differently while the discomfort that usually maintains the loop is still present. One shows how the pattern is reinforced; the other strengthens the capacity to choose values-based action before immediate relief takes over (Baer et al., 1968; Hayes et al., 2012).

To develop it, a person must learn to observe the sequence inside themselves. This is not self-analysis for its own sake. It is practical. Every reaction has a sequence. Something happens. It is perceived. Meaning is assigned. Emotion follows. The body prepares. Behavior becomes likely. Most people become aware near the end of the sequence, when the emotion is already strong and the behavior is already forming. By then, choice is harder. The work is to move awareness earlier.

Instead of noticing only that you are angry, you begin noticing the interpretation that produced the anger. Instead of noticing only that you shut down, you begin noticing the moment when the conversation started to feel overwhelming. Instead of noticing only that you became critical, you begin noticing the fear or disappointment that hardened into criticism. Instead of noticing only that you demanded reassurance, you begin noticing the uncertainty that made reassurance feel urgent. The earlier you can see the sequence, the more influence you have over what happens next.

This is not about blaming yourself for having emotions. Emotions are not moral failures. They are part of the human system. The question is not whether you feel anger, fear, sadness, jealousy, shame, or uncertainty. The question is whether those emotions become the architects of your behavior without your participation. Personal mastery asks you to participate.

It asks you to stop outsourcing your response to the intensity of the moment. It asks you to become intimate with your own patterns, not so you can condemn them, but so you can stop mistaking them for inevitability. It asks you to recognize that your first impulse may be honest, but it may not be wise.

This is especially difficult when the other person has contributed to the pain. People often resist self-examination in those moments because it feels like letting the other person off the hook. If I look at my reaction, will that mean their behavior does not matter? If I regulate myself, will that mean I am accepting what they did? If I speak calmly, will they think the issue is not serious? These fears are understandable, but they confuse regulation with surrender.

You can regulate yourself and still hold someone accountable. You can remain grounded and still name harm clearly. You can speak without escalation and still refuse to minimize what happened. In fact, personal mastery often makes accountability stronger because it prevents the issue from being obscured by your reaction to it.

When your response becomes damaging, the conversation shifts. The original concern gets buried beneath the way you expressed it. The other person now has a reason to focus on your tone, your intensity, your withdrawal, your defensiveness, or you're timing. What needed to be addressed is lost inside the pattern that followed. This does not make their avoidance right. It does show how easily the system can redirect attention away from the real issue.

Personal mastery protects clarity. It allows you to bring a concern without turning the concern into another injury. It allows you to say, "This mattered," without making the other person responsible for surviving the force of your unregulated emotion. It allows you to stay connected to your own dignity while you name what needs to be named.

Dignity is often overlooked in relational conflict. People think the goal is to be right, to be heard, to be reassured, to be vindicated, or to make the other person finally understand. Those goals may contain legitimate needs, but they can also pull a person away from the kind of self they want to bring into love. Dignity asks a different question. Can I remain someone I respect while I am hurting?

This question is not soft. It is demanding. It does not ask you to be agreeable. It does not ask you to hide pain. It does not ask you to carry the relationship alone. It asks whether your behavior under stress reflects your values or merely your activation.

Values are easy to claim when calm. They become meaningful when pressure rises. If you value honesty, can you tell the truth without cruelty? If you value respect, can you remain respectful when you feel misunderstood? If you value emotional safety, can you avoid using vulnerability as a weapon? If you value repair, can you return to the conversation after needing space? If you value accountability, can you acknowledge your impact without first demanding that the other person understand your intention? These are the places where personal mastery becomes visible (Hayes et al., 2012; Ryan & Deci, 2000).

Not in what you believe about yourself, but in what you practice when the relationship touches the part of you that wants to react automatically.

This is why mastery cannot be borrowed from intelligence. A person can be brilliant and still relationally unregulated. They can understand complex systems, lead organizations, manage crises, make strategic decisions, and still become reactive in the intimacy of partnership. Cognitive ability does not guarantee emotional governance. Professional competence does not guarantee relational maturity. In fact, success in other domains can sometimes conceal underdevelopment in love because the skills that produce achievement are not always the skills that sustain intimacy. A person can solve problems and still not know how to be present with pain. They can communicate persuasively and still not know how to listen without preparing a defense. They can perform under pressure and still not know how to soften when closeness requires vulnerability.

Love exposes these differences because it does not only ask what you can accomplish. It asks how you function when another person matters enough to affect you.

That is why relationships are such powerful mirrors. They reveal not only what you want, but how you behave when wanting makes you vulnerable. They reveal what you believe about yourself when someone is disappointed in you. They reveal how you experience another person's need. They reveal whether you interpret difference as threat, whether you confuse control with safety, whether you can tolerate the discomfort of not being immediately understood.

This exposure can feel unfair. It can feel as though the relationship is making you worse, when in fact it may be making visible what was already there. The pattern was not created from nothing. The relationship simply placed it in contact with another person's pattern, and the interaction brought it to the surface. This is where personal mastery requires compassion as well as responsibility.

Without compassion, self-observation turns into self-attack. Every reaction becomes evidence of failure. Every pattern becomes a defect. Every mistake becomes proof that you are not capable of love. This kind of harshness does not produce mastery. It produces shame, and shame often leads to the very behaviors the person is trying to change: defensiveness, withdrawal, collapse, blame, or avoidance. Compassion allows you to look without turning away. Responsibility allows you to change what you see.

Both are necessary. Compassion without responsibility becomes self-excuse. Responsibility without compassion becomes punishment. Personal mastery lives in the balance between the two. It says, "There is a reason I learned this, and there is also a reason I must learn something else." That sentence is one of the most mature positions a person can take in love.

It honors history without being ruled by it. It acknowledges that patterns were formed in context, but it refuses to make context a permanent explanation for harm. It allows growth to occur without requiring self-hatred as the price of change.

The relationship needs that kind of maturity because no system can become healthier if the people inside it cannot tolerate seeing themselves accurately.

Accuracy is threatening when identity is fragile. If a person believes they must be seen as good in order to be safe, then feedback becomes danger. If they believe being wrong means being unworthy, accountability becomes humiliation. If they believe conflict means rejection, disagreement becomes panic. In each case, the relationship cannot discuss what is happening because the discussion itself activates the pattern. Personal mastery strengthens the ability to stay present when identity feels threatened.

It allows a person to hear, "That hurt me," without immediately translating it into, "You are a terrible person." It allows them to hear, "I need something different," without translating it into, "I am not enough." It allows them to hear, "This pattern is not working," without translating it into, "The relationship is failing."

These translations matter because they determine what happens next. If feedback becomes shame, the person will defend against shame instead of understanding impact. If a request becomes criticism, the person will argue with the request instead of considering the need. If another person's pain becomes an accusation, the conversation becomes a trial rather than a repair. The mind is constantly translating. Personal mastery asks you to examine the translation before you react to it.

This is where cognitive discipline enters the work. Not cold analysis, but disciplined attention. What did I hear? What did I assume? What meaning did I add? What does this moment remind me of? What am I protecting right now? What response would serve the relationship rather than simply discharge my discomfort?

These questions are not meant to be recited mechanically in the middle of an argument. They represent a way of training attention. Over time, they become part of how a person relates to their own mind. Instead of treating every interpretation as fact, they begin to hold interpretations with more care. They recognize that an emotional truth may be partial. They become less captured by the first story the mind produces. This is not easy because the first story often feels urgent.

Urgency is one of the great obstacles to personal mastery. When someone feels threatened, the mind insists that action must happen immediately. Send the message. Make the point. Leave the room. Demand the answer. End the conversation. Prove the inconsistency. Correct the misunderstanding. Get reassurance now. The urgency feels like necessity, but often it is discomfort seeking relief. Relief is not the same as repair.

Many relational behaviors are attempts to relieve discomfort. Defensiveness relieves shame. Withdrawal relieves overwhelm. Criticism relieves helplessness. Control relieves uncertainty. Reassurance-seeking relieves fear. Appeasement relieves tension. Each behavior may work briefly, which is why it becomes reinforced. But the relief often comes at the cost of the relationship's long-term stability. Personal mastery asks you to tolerate discomfort long enough to choose something better than immediate relief (Skinner, 1953; Hayes et al., 2006).

This may be one of the most important capacities in love. To stay in the conversation without escalating. To take space without abandoning. To hear pain without collapsing. To admit fault without drowning in shame. To express need without demanding that the other person regulate you instantly. To remain connected to the larger relationship while the moment feels emotionally loud. This is not natural for many people. It has to be practiced.

Practice changes the system. The first time a person pauses instead of defending, the relationship may not transform. The first time they name fear instead of criticizing, the other person may not know how to respond. The first time they return after taking space, trust may not immediately be restored. New behavior often enters an old system awkwardly. It may not be believed at first. It may not be reinforced immediately. It may even be tested by the pattern it is trying to change. This is why personal mastery requires consistency.

A single regulated response is meaningful, but it is not yet a new pattern. A sincere insight matters, but it is not yet trust. The relationship learns from repetition. If the old version of you has been reliable under stress for years, the new version must become reliable enough for the system to believe it. That takes time. It also takes humility (Stokes & Baer, 1977; Baucom et al., 2011).

There is a particular humility required to change in front of someone who has experienced your old pattern. You may want immediate credit for the effort. You may want your partner to notice the restraint, the softer tone, the return, the apology, the attempt to listen. When they do not respond with trust right away, it may feel unfair. You may think, I am trying. Why is that not enough? Trying matters. But trust responds to demonstrated pattern, not isolated effort.

If someone has been hurt by repeated withdrawal, they may not relax the first time you stay. If someone has experienced repeated defensiveness, they may not feel safe after one accountable conversation. If someone has lived with inconsistency, they may not believe consistency until it has survived inconvenience. Their caution is not always a refusal to see your growth. Sometimes it is the system remembering what it has learned. Personal mastery includes tolerating that lag.

It means becoming more committed to the new pattern than to being immediately rewarded for it. It means understanding that change is not fully yours until it persists without applause. It means allowing the relationship time to update its expectations. This is where the work becomes less performative and more real.

Anyone can behave differently for a moment when the motivation is high, the stakes are obvious, or the relationship is on the line. The deeper question is whether the new behavior remains when the urgency fades. Does the person return to old patterns once the immediate crisis passes? Does accountability continue when the conversation is less dramatic? Does regulation remain when the relationship is not actively being threatened? Personal mastery is proven in ordinary repetition.

It is built in the daily moments where old patterns could easily reappear: the tired response at the end of a long day, the small disappointment, the minor correction, the request that arrives at an inconvenient time, the conversation that begins when no one has much energy left. These are the moments that shape the system more than people realize. They teach the relationship what is dependable. Dependability is one of the quietest forms of love.

Not dependability as rigid predictability, where a person becomes controlled, flat, or emotionally unavailable. Dependability as relational trustworthiness. The other person begins to know that even when you are frustrated, you will not become cruel. Even when you need space, you will return. Even when you disagree, you will not punish. Even when you are ashamed, you will not make accountability impossible. Even when the conversation is hard, you will not abandon the relationship emotionally simply because discomfort has arrived. This is what it means to become someone who can stay.

Staying is not merely physical presence. Many people remain in the room while disappearing internally. They shut down, comply, detach, or wait for the conversation to end. Others stay physically but become emotionally unsafe through anger, contempt, criticism, or relentless pressure. Real staying is different. It is the ability to remain engaged without losing yourself and without turning the other person into the enemy. To stay is to remain available to the truth of the moment.

That truth may include your pain. It may include the other person's pain. It may include your responsibility, their responsibility, or the recognition that both of you are participating in a pattern that neither of you wants. Staying means resisting the impulse to escape into the familiar roles: victim, prosecutor, defendant, rescuer, judge, ghost. It means remaining human in a moment when the system is trying to make you automatic.

This is not always possible in the moment. Sometimes the body is too activated. Sometimes a pause is necessary. Sometimes the wisest act is to say, "I cannot do this well right now, and I need to come back to it." That can be personal mastery too, if the space is used for regulation rather than avoidance, and if return is part of the commitment. Taking space without return is abandonment of the process. Taking space with return can be care.

The difference is structure. If one person leaves a conversation because they are overwhelmed and never reopens it, the system learns that difficult topics disappear into silence. If they take space, regulate, and return with clarity, the system learns that intensity does not have to become rupture. Over time, this teaches both people that difficult moments can be survived without being forced or avoided. That is a profound shift.

Many people have never experienced conflict that ends in deeper understanding. They have experienced conflict that ends in exhaustion, distance, apology without change, or a temporary return to normal. Personal mastery helps create the conditions for something different. It allows conflict to become less of a battlefield and more of a point of information. Not painless, not easy, but usable. This requires the ability to separate feeling from action.

A feeling may be immediate. Action does not have to be. A feeling may be intense. Action can still be chosen. A feeling may be valid. Action may still need to be revised. This separation is central to maturity because without it, every emotional state becomes a command. Anger says attack. Fear says control. Shame says defend. Anxiety says pursue. Overwhelm says disappear.

Personal mastery says, "I hear the command. I do not have to obey it." That sentence, lived consistently, changes a relationship.

It does not make a person passive. It makes them more deliberate. They may still express anger, but without contempt. They may still name fear, but without accusation. They may still set boundaries, but without punishment. They may still ask for reassurance, but without making the other person responsible for erasing every insecurity. They may still need space, but without using silence as a weapon. The emotion remains. The behavior changes. When behavior changes consistently, the system begins to change with it.

This is where personal mastery connects back to systems thinking. The self is not separate from the system. The self is one of the system's most important inputs. Every time you respond differently, you introduce different information into the relationship. You do not control the entire outcome, but you alter the conditions. You make the old sequence less inevitable. This is the only place relational change can honestly begin.

Not because the other person does not need to change. They may. Not because the system can be transformed by one person alone. Often it cannot. But because the self is the part of the system you can access directly. You cannot regulate another person into maturity. You cannot force their curiosity, humility, accountability, or repair. You cannot make them see the pattern if they are invested in not seeing it. But you can decide whether you will continue to feed the pattern in the same way.

That decision may change the relationship. It may reveal that the relationship can learn. It may invite a different response from the other person and create a new sequence between you. It may begin the slow process of rebuilding trust. Or it may reveal the limits of the relationship.

Sometimes personal mastery clarifies that you are the only one doing the work. As you become more regulated, more honest, and more willing to examine your part, it may become painfully clear that the system remains unchanged because the other person is unwilling or unable to participate. That clarity matters. Personal mastery is not a tool for carrying the entire relational burden more gracefully. It is a way of seeing accurately, acting responsibly, and making decisions from a more grounded place. A relationship cannot become a learning system through one person's mastery alone. But one person's mastery can reveal whether learning is possible.

That revelation is not always the one people want. Sometimes it shows that the relationship has more capacity than either person realized. Sometimes it shows that love is present but the structure is still immature. Sometimes it shows that affection cannot compensate for a lack of accountability. Sometimes it shows that the healthiest change is not staying in the same pattern with better language, but stepping out of a system that cannot or will not become safe enough to grow. In every case, personal mastery gives the individual a different relationship to themselves.

They are no longer simply carried by reaction. They become more able to observe, choose, repair, and decide. They become less dependent on the other person's behavior to determine whether they remain aligned with their own values. They become less likely to confuse intensity with truth, urgency with necessity, or self-protection with wisdom. This changes the emotional architecture of love.

When two people develop personal mastery, the relationship gains stability from the inside. Not because conflict disappears, but because conflict no longer automatically disorganizes the system. Both people can bring themselves back into the conversation. Both can notice when old patterns are taking over. Both can take responsibility without collapsing. Both can make room for the possibility that their first interpretation is not the whole truth. The relationship becomes less reactive because the people inside it become less automatic. This is the beginning of a more mature partnership.

Not a perfect partnership. Not a relationship where both people always respond well, always regulate quickly, or always know what to do. Personal mastery does not create emotional perfection. It creates recoverability. The ability to notice sooner, repair more honestly, return more reliably, and learn from what happened instead of simply repeating it. Recoverability may be more important than harmony.

Harmony is often temporary. It depends on conditions being favorable, needs being met, and tension remaining low. Recoverability is deeper. It allows the relationship to survive moments when harmony is disrupted. It gives the system a way back from strain. It tells both people that difficulty does not have to become destruction. But recoverability requires someone to pause before the old pattern takes over. Someone has to notice. Someone has to choose differently. Someone has to remain connected to the larger relationship when the immediate emotion is demanding control. That someone, for each person, can only be themselves.

This is the one thing you cannot avoid. You can study the pattern. You can understand the system. You can identify the loops, the reinforcements, the assumptions, and the recurring conflicts. But eventually the work arrives at the self. At your reaction. Your interpretation. Your tone. Your silence. Your timing. Your willingness to repair. Your ability to stay present when the system becomes stressful. The relationship may be larger than you, but you are not outside it. You are one of the ways it becomes what it becomes.

Personal mastery is the decision to become conscious of that fact before the pattern decides for you. It is the discipline of bringing your values into the moments where your history would rather take over. It is the practice of becoming someone who can feel deeply without being ruled entirely by feeling, someone who can hurt without immediately harming, someone who can be afraid without making fear the architect of the relationship. That kind of person changes the system simply by entering it differently. Not all at once. Not perfectly. But enough to make a new pattern possible.

CHAPTER FIVE

MENTAL MODELS

The Invisible Rules Running Your Relationship

A relationship does not only respond to what happens. It responds to what each person believes has happened.

That distinction is easy to miss because belief often arrives disguised as reality. A tone is heard, and meaning appears almost immediately. A silence occurs, and the mind begins to explain it. A request is made, and before the other person has finished speaking, the relationship is already being interpreted through a private set of assumptions about what requests mean, what tone means, what silence means, what love should do, and what danger looks like when it enters the room. Most people do not experience this as interpretation. They experience it as knowing.

They know when someone is pulling away. They know when a partner is disappointed. They know when a question is really criticism, when quietness is really distance, when a disagreement is really rejection, when a need is really pressure, when a boundary is really punishment. The conclusion feels immediate because the mind does not announce the process by which it arrived there. It simply presents the result.

This is one of the reasons relationships become so difficult to understand from inside them. Two people may be responding not only to each other, but to the invisible rules each has learned about what the other person's behavior means. They may believe they are arguing about the present moment, when they are also arguing through old assumptions, inherited beliefs, prior disappointments, and internal predictions that have been built over time. These invisible rules are mental models.

Cognitive psychology and ACT describe this problem in complementary ways. Cognitive theory draws attention to the automatic appraisals, distortions, and attributions that shape emotion before deliberate reflection has occurred. ACT adds that people can become fused with these interpretations, treating a thought as reality rather than as one possible construction of reality. In relationships, fusion turns "I am having the thought that I am being rejected" into "I am being rejected," and the system begins responding to the interpretation as though it were fact (Beck, 1976; Bradbury & Fincham, 1990; Hayes et al., 2006).

A mental model is the internal framework through which a person understands reality. It is a map, but not the territory itself. It organizes experience. It tells the mind what to notice, what to ignore, what to expect, and what to fear. It helps simplify the world so that every situation does not have to be interpreted from nothing. Without mental models, life would be overwhelming. Every tone, gesture, silence, conflict, and expression of affection would have to be evaluated from the beginning, without reference or pattern. The mind does not work that way. It uses what it has learned (Senge, 2006; Beck, 1976; Kahneman, 2011).

The problem is not that mental models exist. They are necessary. The problem is that most people treat them as reality rather than as interpretations of reality. They forget that the map was drawn from a particular history. They forget that what feels obvious may have been learned in an environment that is no longer present. They forget that the meaning their mind assigns may be emotionally powerful and still incomplete.

In relationships, this matters because mental models do not remain private. They become relational. They shape how a person listens, reacts, asks, withdraws, defends, apologizes, forgives, and interprets the other person's behavior. They influence the system before either person realizes the system has been influenced.

One person hears silence and thinks, They are shutting me out. Another hears silence and thinks, We are giving each other space. One person experiences directness as honesty. Another experiences the same directness as aggression.

One person sees frequent reassurance as love. Another sees the need for reassurance as lack of trust. One person believes conflict means the relationship is in danger. Another believes conflict means the relationship is finally telling the truth. Neither person is merely responding to the event. Each is responding through a model.

This is why two people can live through the same interaction and emerge with entirely different accounts of what happened. One says, "I was just trying to talk." The other says, "You were attacking me." One says, "I needed a minute." The other says, "You abandoned the conversation." One says, "I was being honest." The other says, "You were being cruel." Both are certain because each is describing the interaction from within the model that organized their experience. The certainty is sincere. That does not make it complete.

Human beings are not neutral observers of their relationships. They do not simply record what happens and respond to it with clean objectivity. They perceive through expectation. They interpret through memory. They assign meaning through frameworks shaped by family, culture, prior relationships, attachment, disappointment, longing, and fear. By the time a reaction becomes visible, the mind has already done a great deal of work beneath awareness (Tversky & Kahneman, 1974; Bradbury & Fincham, 1990).

This is why a small moment can carry disproportionate force. The delayed response is not only a delayed response if the person receiving it carries a model that says love is proven by responsiveness. The request for space is not only a request for space if the person hearing it carries a model that says distance means rejection. The disagreement is not only disagreement if one person carries a model that says conflict leads to abandonment or humiliation. The moment is filtered through a system of meaning. Once meaning is assigned, emotion follows. Once emotion follows, behavior begins to organize around it.

A person who believes silence means abandonment will not respond to silence in the same way as someone who believes silence means regulation. A person who believes criticism is coming will not hear feedback in the same way as someone who believes feedback is part of repair. A person who believes needs make them burdensome will not ask for care in the same way as someone who believes needs can be spoken without shame. Mental models shape the emotional weather of the relationship. They also shape what is possible inside it.

If your model says love should not require direct explanation, then asking clearly for what you need may feel like evidence that the relationship is already failing. If your model says your partner should know what matters without being told, then communication becomes less about clarity and more about testing. If your model says conflict means danger, then every difficult conversation becomes something to avoid, manage, or survive. If your model says vulnerability will be used against you, then intimacy becomes desirable in theory and threatening in practice. These models are rarely chosen deliberately. They are built.

A child who grows up in a home where anger leads to withdrawal may learn that conflict causes disappearance. A child who grows up around explosive arguments may learn that disagreement is unsafe, even when no one says those words directly. A child who is praised for independence may learn that needing others is weakness. A child whose emotions are dismissed may learn to overstate pain in order to be taken seriously, or to hide it entirely because expression seems useless.

A person who has been betrayed may develop a model in which trust is always provisional. A person who has been controlled may experience ordinary requests as threats to autonomy. A person who has been neglected may interpret inconsistency quickly and painfully. A person who has been criticized repeatedly may hear correction as contempt, even when contempt is not present. These are not random reactions. They are learned ways of organizing experience.

The difficulty is that what was learned for protection may later interfere with connection. A mental model that once helped a person anticipate danger may become so sensitive that it mistakes difference for threat. A model that once encouraged self-reliance may make mutual dependence feel unbearable. A model that once protected someone from humiliation may make honest feedback nearly impossible to receive. This is why mental models deserve compassion, but not unquestioned loyalty.

There is usually a reason they formed. There is usually a history that made them feel necessary. They may have helped someone survive a family system, a previous relationship, a period of instability, or a repeated pattern of disappointment. But a model built in one environment may not serve the relationship being built now. The fact that an interpretation has a history does not mean it should govern the present without examination. A relationship cannot mature beyond the models that run it unconsciously.

This becomes especially clear when two people use the same language but live inside different meanings. They may both say they value communication, yet one believes communication means talking about emotional experience as it happens, while the other believes communication means addressing problems once they can be discussed calmly. One person feels neglected by the delay. The other feels pressured by the immediacy. Both value communication. Neither has defined the model behind the word.

They may both say they value respect. For one, respect means being direct enough not to hide the truth. For the other, respect means being careful enough not to harm the other person with the truth. One feels disrespected by avoidance. The other feels disrespected by bluntness. The value is shared at the level of language, but divided at the level of practice.

They may both say they value loyalty. One defines loyalty as visible prioritization, emotional reassurance, and protection from outside influence. The other defines loyalty as reliability, privacy, and continuing to show up even without constant verbal affirmation. Both may believe they are loyal. Both may feel the other is failing. The conflict is not always about whether the value exists. It is about the model through which the value is understood.

Undefined values become invisible rules. Invisible rules become unmet expectations. Unmet expectations become interpretations. Interpretations become emotional reactions. Emotional reactions become behavior. Behavior becomes the system. This is how mental models quietly become relational architecture. They build without asking permission.

The most dangerous mental models are not always the dramatic ones. Often, they are the ones that sound reasonable. "If they cared, they would make time." "If I mattered, they would notice." "If this were right, it would not be this hard." "If they loved me, I would not have to explain." "If we were compatible, we would not keep having this conversation."

Each statement contains a possible truth. Care does require time. Love does involve attention. Compatibility should reduce some forms of friction. A partner who repeatedly ignores clearly expressed needs may reveal something important. But the danger lies in turning these partial truths into absolute rules. Once a rule becomes absolute, curiosity disappears. The mind stops investigating. It starts confirming.

Confirmation is one of the mind's most powerful habits. Once a person believes a partner is distant, selfish, critical, careless, controlling, or emotionally unavailable, the mind begins noticing evidence that supports the belief. Contradictory evidence may be minimized or explained away. Supportive behavior becomes an exception. Ambiguous behavior becomes proof. A neutral moment becomes suspicious because the model is already prepared to interpret it. This does not happen because the person is irrational. It happens because the mind seeks coherence (Tversky & Kahneman, 1974; Kahneman, 2011).

A coherent story feels safer than uncertainty. It is easier to live inside a painful explanation than to live inside ambiguity. If the mind can decide what is happening, it can prepare a response. It can defend, withdraw, pursue, appease, or control. Uncertainty leaves the system open. For many people, openness feels less safe than being wrong with conviction. Mental models therefore do more than interpret the relationship. They protect the person from the discomfort of not knowing. But love requires the capacity not to know too quickly.

This may be one of the hardest forms of relational maturity: the ability to hold an interpretation without becoming immediately loyal to it. To notice the thought, They do not care, and pause long enough to ask whether care is truly absent or whether disappointment has narrowed the field of vision. To notice the thought, They are attacking me, and ask whether the moment contains criticism, concern, clumsiness, or pain. To notice the thought, I am not safe, and distinguish between real danger, emotional discomfort, and the activation of an old model. This is not self-doubt for its own sake. It is disciplined perception (Hayes et al., 2006; Hayes et al., 2012).

Disciplined perception does not mean ignoring red flags, explaining away harmful behavior, or forcing yourself to reinterpret what is clearly damaging. Some behaviors are exactly what they appear to be. Contempt, manipulation, chronic dishonesty, repeated boundary violations, betrayal, and emotional cruelty should not be softened by endless interpretive generosity. A mature understanding of mental models does not ask people to mistrust their own experience in order to preserve a relationship. It asks them to become precise.

Precision is different from suspicion, and it is different from denial. Precision asks: what happened, what did I make it mean, what evidence supports that meaning, what history may be influencing my interpretation, and what response would serve clarity rather than simply serve the model? The difference between feeling and meaning becomes essential here.

A feeling is real because it is experienced. If you feel hurt, the hurt is real. If you feel afraid, the fear is real. If you feel dismissed, the feeling of dismissal is real. But the meaning attached to the feeling may require examination. Feeling dismissed does not always mean the other person intended dismissal. Feeling abandoned does not always mean abandonment is occurring. Feeling controlled does not always mean the request was controlling. Feeling criticized does not always mean the feedback was contemptuous. This distinction is not meant to invalidate emotion. It is meant to protect the relationship from being governed by unexamined meaning.

In cognitive terms, people often treat emotion as evidence. If I feel rejected, I must have been rejected. If I feel unsafe, danger must be present. If I feel guilty, I must have done something wrong. If I feel uncertain, the relationship must be unstable. This emotional reasoning can be powerful because it seems to honor experience. But honoring experience does not require surrendering to the first explanation the experience produces. Emotions tell us that something matters. They do not always tell us what is true (Beck, 1976; Beck et al., 1979).

A person can feel fear because danger is present, or because intimacy has moved close enough to activate old protection. A person can feel anger because a boundary was crossed, or because a need was not expressed until resentment had accumulated. A person can feel guilty because they caused harm, or because they set a necessary boundary in a system that equates boundaries with rejection. The feeling deserves attention. The meaning deserves inquiry.

When inquiry is absent, distortion becomes more likely. The mind may catastrophize, turning a difficult conversation into evidence that the relationship is doomed. It may personalize, interpreting another person's stress as a statement about one's worth. It may mind-read, assuming knowledge of the other person's motive without asking. It may turn one moment into an entire identity: You were late; therefore, you are unreliable; you disagreed; therefore, you do not respect me; you needed space; therefore, you do not love me (Beck, 1976; Bradbury & Fincham, 1990).

These distortions are not character flaws. They are cognitive shortcuts. Under stress, the mind moves quickly. It simplifies. It protects. It reaches for familiar conclusions because familiar conclusions require less energy than careful understanding. The more emotionally charged the relationship, the more powerful these shortcuts become. This is why mental models are most visible under pressure.

When the relationship feels calm, many models remain dormant. A person may believe they are open, trusting, generous, and secure. Under favorable conditions, that may be true enough. But when ambiguity enters, the model begins to speak. When a partner is unavailable, when a disagreement emerges, when desire changes, when attention shifts, when stress enters the system, the invisible rules become active. What does this mean? What does this say about us? What does this say about me? The answer that arrives is often less about the moment than about the model.

If the model says love is proven by constant attention, then any decrease in attention will feel like emotional danger. If the model says conflict predicts abandonment, then even healthy disagreement will feel threatening. If the model says needs are too much, then asking for care will feel humiliating. If the model says independence equals strength, then reliance on a partner will feel like weakness. The model defines the threat. Then the person responds to the threat as though it is objective.

This is how relationships become trapped in reactions that seem reasonable from the inside and confusing from the outside. One partner says, "I did not do anything wrong." The other says, "You should have known what that meant to me." Both may be telling the truth from within their own model. One is describing the event. The other is describing the meaning. Until the difference is visible, the conversation cannot move. It remains stuck in competing realities.

Competing realities are among the most exhausting experiences in a relationship. Each person feels certain. Each person feels misunderstood. Each person believes the other is refusing to acknowledge what is obvious. The conversation becomes less about the original issue and more about whose reality will be accepted. This is where many couples begin to lose each other. Not because the issue is impossible, but because neither person has learned to speak from the level of the model.

To speak from the level of the model is to say something more revealing than, "You ignored me." It is to say, "When I did not hear from you, my mind went to the place where I assume I am not important." It is different from saying, "You are attacking me." It is to say, "When your voice gets direct, I start hearing criticism even before I know whether that is what you mean." It is different from saying, "You do not care." It is to say, "I have a model of care that depends heavily on visible follow-through, and when that is missing, I struggle to feel secure." This kind of language does not excuse the other person from responding well. It makes response possible.

When the model is named, the relationship gains access to information that accusation usually hides. The other person can begin to understand not only what hurt, but why it carried the meaning it did. The conversation shifts from defending against a charge to understanding a pattern of interpretation. This does not guarantee agreement. It does create a different kind of space.

The same is true in reverse. If one person says, "You never let me breathe," the conversation may become defensive immediately. But if they can say, "When I feel pressure to resolve something before I am ready, I start experiencing the conversation as control, even if I know you are seeking closeness," the relationship has more to work with. The statement reveals the model without making the other person the villain inside it.

This is not easy. It requires personal mastery because mental models often feel most convincing precisely when they need to be examined. It requires enough regulation to slow the mind's first conclusion. It requires enough humility to acknowledge that one's interpretation may be shaped by more than the present moment. It requires enough courage to reveal the vulnerable rule beneath the reaction.

Many people prefer to argue at the level of behavior because behavior feels safer. It is easier to say, "You did not text me back," than to say, "When I do not hear from you, I become afraid that I am becoming less important." It is easier to say, "Stop criticizing me," than to say, "I do not know how to hear disappointment without feeling like I have failed as a person." It is easier to say,

"You are too needy," than to say, "I am afraid that if I let your needs matter, I will disappear inside them."

Behavior matters. It must be discussed. But beneath behavior are meanings, and beneath meanings are models. If the conversation never reaches that level, the couple may keep rearranging the surface while the deeper structure remains intact.

This is why the work of changing mental models is not merely an intellectual exercise. It is relational work. It changes how two people make meaning together. It helps them understand where their interpretations are aligned, where they are not, and where the system is being governed by assumptions neither has named. The first step is not to discard every model. The first step is to see them.

A person might begin to notice that they assume silence means punishment. That they interpret a partner's independence as lack of desire. That they equate disagreement with disrespect. That they believe love should be intuitive and therefore feel ashamed when they have to ask directly for what they need. That they treat emotional intensity as proof of depth. That they feel safer being needed than being truly known.

These recognitions can be uncomfortable because they reveal how much of the relationship has been shaped by rules that were never consciously chosen. But they also create freedom. What can be seen can be questioned. What can be questioned can be revised. What can be revised no longer has to run the system from the background. Revision does not mean replacing one rigid model with another. It means developing more flexible understanding.

A rigid model says, "If they need space, they are pulling away." A more flexible model says, "Space can mean withdrawal, regulation, avoidance, or care, and I need to understand which one is happening here." A rigid model says, "If we fight, something is wrong." A more flexible model says, "Conflict can signal danger, but it can also signal difference, unmet needs, or the need for clearer structure." A rigid model says, "If I have to ask, it does not count." A more flexible model says, "Clear requests are not evidence of failure; they are part of building a relationship that does not rely on mind reading." Flexibility is not weakness. It is accuracy under complexity.

Relationships require that kind of accuracy because two people will never share identical histories, identical nervous systems, identical meanings, or identical rules for love. Even when they are well matched, they are still interpreting from different maps. A mature relationship does not require those maps to be identical. It requires both people to know they are using maps at all.

Once that is understood, difference becomes less threatening. The goal is no longer to prove that one model is right and the other is wrong. The goal is to understand how each model operates, what it protects, what it distorts, and what the relationship needs in order to function more clearly. This is where curiosity becomes a structural strength.

Curiosity interrupts certainty. It asks what else might be true. It does not erase impact, but it makes room for understanding before the pattern becomes automatic. A curious person can say, "This is what I am making it mean, but I want to check before I respond from that place." A curious partner can ask, "When I went quiet, what did that mean to you?" or "When you asked for reassurance, what were you afraid was happening?" These questions change the system because they slow the movement from interpretation to reaction. They invite both people into the space between event and meaning. That space is where the relationship becomes more intelligent.

Without it, the system is driven by assumption. With it, the system begins to learn. Each person starts to understand not only what the other does, but how the other makes meaning. Patterns that once felt personal begin to become legible. The partner is no longer only the person who withdraws, criticizes, pursues, questions, or hesitates. They become a person operating through a model that can be understood, challenged, and revised. This does not mean every model deserves accommodation.

Some models are too damaging to organize a relationship around. A model that equates love with control will injure the system. A model that treats accountability as humiliation will prevent repair. A model that sees vulnerability as weakness will limit intimacy. A model that defines loyalty as unquestioned agreement will punish honesty. Understanding these models does not mean accepting them as reasonable terms for love. Understanding clarifies what must change.

A relationship can only adapt around a model for so long before the adaptation becomes distortion. One person can be careful with another's sensitivity, but if every concern is interpreted as attack, the relationship will become silent. One person can respect another's need for independence, but if independence becomes a refusal to be affected by the relationship, partnership will never fully form. One person can offer reassurance, but if reassurance becomes the only way the other person regulates fear, the relationship will become responsible for managing what the individual has not learned to hold. Mental models must be examined not only for where they came from, but for what they produce. That is the systems question.

What does this model make more likely? Does it create clarity or confusion? Does it increase safety or avoidance? Does it invite repair or defensiveness? Does it allow both people to remain whole, or does it require one person to shrink so the other can feel secure? The answers matter because models become self-fulfilling when they go unexamined.

A person who believes they will be abandoned may protest, test, monitor, and demand reassurance in ways that create exhaustion and distance. When distance appears, the model feels confirmed. A person who believes conflict is unsafe may avoid difficult conversations until resentment builds. When the delayed conversation finally erupts, the model feels confirmed. A person who believes others cannot be trusted may withhold, investigate, and control until intimacy becomes impossible. When the relationship weakens, the model feels confirmed. The model creates the conditions that prove it right.

This is one of the most painful ways people repeat relational history. They do not simply find the same outcome. They participate in recreating the conditions under which that outcome becomes more likely. Not because they want it, and not because they are to blame for everything that happens, but because unconscious models organize behavior toward familiar conclusions. This is why seeing the model matters. It interrupts repetition at the level where repetition begins.

A person who notices the abandonment model can begin to ask for reassurance without testing the relationship. A person who notices the conflict model can begin to take space and return rather than disappear. A person who notices the mistrust model can distinguish between actual evidence and old expectation. A person who notices the self-protection model can begin to let the present relationship be different from the one that taught them to guard themselves. This is not quick work.

Mental models do not change because they are named once. They change through repeated experiences that challenge them safely and consistently enough for the mind to update its expectations. A person who believes conflict means abandonment must experience conflict followed by repair many times before the model begins to loosen. A person who believes needs are dangerous must experience needs being heard without punishment. A person who believes honesty leads to rejection must experience truth being held with steadiness. The system has to teach the mind something new. But the mind must be willing to learn.

This is where two forms of learning meet: individual learning and relational learning. Individually, each person must become aware of their models, question their interpretations, and practice more flexible responses. Relationally, both people must create enough safety and consistency for new models to become believable. If one person tries to revise a model while the relationship keeps reinforcing the old one, change becomes difficult. If someone is trying to believe that honesty is safe but honesty is repeatedly punished, the old model will remain stronger because the system continues to validate it. This is why mental models cannot be addressed only through insight. They must be addressed through pattern.

A person may understand that their fear of rejection is old. That insight matters, but if the relationship repeatedly responds to vulnerability with impatience or dismissal, the fear will not soften. A person may understand that their defensiveness comes from shame. That insight matters, but if accountability continues to be delivered with contempt, the defensive model will remain activated. Insight opens the door. Repeated relational experience teaches the body whether it is safe to walk through it.

This is also why one person cannot do all the interpretive work for the relationship. It is generous to understand your partner's history. It is valuable to recognize the model beneath their reaction. But if that understanding becomes a reason to absorb harm, silence your needs, or continually accommodate patterns that are not being examined by the other person, the relationship does not become wiser. It becomes imbalanced. Compassion must be paired with accountability.

A model can explain why someone reacts strongly. It does not grant permission for that reaction to damage the relationship indefinitely. A model can explain why someone withdraws. It does not make disappearance a sustainable form of conflict management. A model can explain why someone seeks reassurance. It does not make constant reassurance-seeking the other person's permanent responsibility. The goal is not to worship the model. The goal is to revise it in service of a healthier system.

That revision often begins with a simple but demanding practice: separating observation from interpretation. Observation says, "You were quiet after dinner." Interpretation says, "You were angry with me." Observation says, "You asked to pause the conversation." Interpretation says, "You were avoiding accountability." Observation says, "You disagreed with my decision." Interpretation says, "You do not respect me."

The interpretation may be accurate. It may not be. The point is not to deny it. The point is to recognize that it has been added. Once it is recognized as added, it can be checked. The relationship gains a chance to clarify before reacting to a conclusion that may have been incomplete.

This practice changes communication. Instead of saying, "You shut me out," a person may say, "When you got quiet, I interpreted it as you shutting me out. Is that what was happening?" Instead of saying, "You do not care," they may say, "When this was not followed through on, I made it mean that it was not important to you, and that hurt." Instead of saying, "You are trying to control me," they may say, "I am experiencing this request as control, and I want to understand whether that is your intention or my reaction." This kind of language requires maturity because it gives up the immediate power of accusation. It also creates a greater possibility of truth.

Accusation often produces defense. Interpretation stated as interpretation invites clarification. It still names impact. It still holds the seriousness of the moment. But it does not force the other person to begin by disproving a conclusion. It allows the relationship to examine meaning before becoming organized around it.

Over time, this builds a different kind of trust. Not the trust that neither person will ever misunderstand the other, but the trust that misunderstandings can be brought into the open before they become permanent stories. The relationship becomes less vulnerable to private conclusions. It becomes more capable of checking its own assumptions. That capability is central to becoming a learning relationship.

A relationship that cannot question its models will repeat them. A relationship that can question them begins to evolve. It starts to see that some conflicts are not about the immediate topic but about the rules beneath the topic. It learns that some emotional reactions are not evidence of present danger but signals that an old model has been activated. It learns that some differences are not incompatibilities but untranslated assumptions. This does not make every conflict solvable. It makes the real conflict more visible.

Sometimes the real conflict is not, "You never communicate." It is, "We have different models of what communication is for." Sometimes it is not, "You are not committed." It is, "We express and recognize commitment through different behaviors." Sometimes it is not, "You are too sensitive." It is, "Your system detects threat quickly, and my way of responding has not created enough safety or clarity." Sometimes it is not, "You do not care about my needs." It is, "I have not made my needs understandable, and you have not learned how to respond to them consistently." The shift from accusation to model does not reduce seriousness. It deepens it.

It allows the relationship to address the structure rather than endlessly litigating the surface. It gives both people a chance to ask what rules they are living by, whether those rules were ever agreed upon, and whether those rules are helping them build the relationship they actually want. This is the beginning of shared consciousness.

Two people stop assuming that love should automatically mean the same thing to both of them. They stop treating their own definitions as universal. They begin to see that every relationship is partly an act of translation. What does closeness mean to you? What does respect look like when we disagree? What does repair require after harm? What does loyalty demand, and what does it not demand? What does space mean? What does silence mean? What does commitment look like on an ordinary day when no one is performing devotion? These questions are not merely philosophical. They are practical.

A relationship lives through definitions that become behavior. If those definitions remain invisible, the relationship will be governed by assumptions. If they become visible, they can be negotiated, refined, and aligned. The couple does not have to share identical histories, but they do need shared understanding. They do not need the same first reaction, but they need a way to interpret reactions accurately enough that they do not become trapped inside them. This is where seeing the other person becomes possible in a new way.

Before mental models are examined, people often see their partner through the role the model assigns. The withdrawer. The critic. The needy one. The distant one. The controlling one. The selfish one. The dramatic one. These roles may be built from real behaviors, but once they harden, they begin to obscure the person underneath. The partner becomes less a human being in the present and more a character inside a familiar story. Mental models turn people into evidence. Awareness turns them back into people.

To see someone more clearly is not to idealize them. It is not to ignore their behavior or excuse their impact. It is to distinguish between the person, the pattern, and the meaning your mind has added. It is to recognize that the partner in front of you may be more complex than the role they occupy in your model. They may be afraid where you saw indifference. Overwhelmed where you saw refusal. Ashamed where you saw arrogance. Trying poorly where you saw not trying at all. Again, this does not excuse harm. It makes understanding more accurate.

Accuracy matters because love cannot mature inside caricature. A relationship cannot become healthier when each person is interacting with a simplified version of the other. The system needs enough truth to change, and truth requires seeing not only what the other person does, but how both people have come to understand what it means. This is the deeper purpose of examining mental models.

Not to become endlessly analytical. Not to turn every feeling into an investigation. Not to make love cautious, intellectualized, or detached. The purpose is to create enough awareness that the relationship is no longer run entirely by invisible rules. Feeling remains. Instinct remains. Emotion remains. But they are joined by curiosity, humility, and the capacity to revise. A mature relationship does not ask either person to abandon their inner world. It asks them to stop mistaking their inner world for the whole relationship.

Your model may be telling you something important. It may be identifying a real wound, a real need, a real boundary, or a real pattern that deserves attention. It may also be repeating a story that no longer deserves the authority it has been given. The task is not to silence it. The task is to bring it into consciousness, test it against the present, and decide whether it helps the relationship become more honest, safer, and more capable. This is where love becomes less automatic and more intentional.

A person begins to hear their own interpretations differently. They notice the old rule before it becomes the old reaction. They begin to say, "This is what my mind is making of this," rather than, "This is simply what is true." They become more willing to ask, "What else could be happening?" They learn to speak from vulnerability before accusation, and from clarity before defense. When both people can do this, the relationship gains a new kind of strength.

Not the strength of perfect understanding, but the strength of shared inquiry. The ability to pause inside a misunderstanding and examine the meaning before the meaning becomes a wound. The ability to recognize that love is not only affected by what happens, but by the interpretations that follow what happens. The ability to revise the rules that no longer serve the relationship being built. This is the final movement of Part II.

First, the relationship had to be seen as a system. Then the self-had to be seen inside that system. Now the mind itself must be seen as part of the system, because the mind is constantly assigning meaning to love. It is constantly building reality from fragments of behavior, memory, and expectation. If that process remains unconscious, the relationship will be governed by stories neither person has chosen deliberately. But when the process becomes visible, something changes.

The delayed response can be checked before it becomes rejection. The difficult conversation can be entered before it becomes danger. The need can be named before it becomes resentment. The silence can be clarified before it becomes a verdict. The partner can be seen before they are turned into a symbol of every old fear. This does not make love simple. It makes it more truthful.

And truth is what the relationship will need as it moves beyond the illusion, beyond the first recognition of the system, and into the deeper patterns that unfold over time. Because once two people begin to understand the rules they have been living by, they are ready to see the cycle those rules have helped create. The relationship has a pattern. The next question is how that pattern moves.

PART III
THE PATTERN

Once the system becomes visible, time begins to matter differently.

A relationship is not only shaped by what two people feel, what they believe, or how they respond in isolated moments. It is shaped by how those responses unfold over time. Love has movement. It develops, accelerates, settles, strains, adapts, or repeats. What seems like a sudden change is often the visible stage of a cycle that has been turning for much longer than either person recognized. Part III turns toward that movement.

The first two parts of this book challenged the illusion that love succeeds because it feels right and introduced the system beneath the feeling. But systems do not remain still. They evolve under pressure. They respond to stress, expectation, disappointment, and routine. They reveal themselves not only in arguments, but in the quiet changes that occur when the early conditions of love begin to shift.

This is where many people become confused. They assume that the relationship has changed because the feeling has changed. They assume distance means loss, conflict means incompatibility, and effort means something has gone wrong. But often the relationship is not ending. It is entering a different phase, one that requires capacities the beginning did not demand.

Chapter 6, "The Cycle of Love," examines the predictable movement from early intensity into exposure. It looks at how relationships begin with momentum, why ease can be mistaken for strength, and how the first slowing of that momentum often reveals the structure that was never fully built.

Chapter 7, "The Shift from Me to Us," explores one of the most important transitions in any serious relationship: the movement from two individuals managing themselves beside each other to two people learning how to function as a team. This shift is often assumed, but rarely automatic.

Chapter 8, "What Love Is Actually Made Of," widens the frame. Once feeling, connection, chemistry, and commitment are understood as necessary but incomplete, the question becomes more precise. What is love actually made of when it has to function under real conditions?

The purpose of this section is not to reduce love to stages or formulas. Human relationships are too complex for that. The purpose is to make the pattern visible enough that the reader can recognize where they are inside it. A relationship that feels confusing from within often becomes more understandable when its movement is seen over time. Love does not fail only in dramatic ruptures. Sometimes it fails because no one recognized the cycle until the cycle had already done its work.

CHAPTER SIX

THE CYCLE OF LOVE

The Wheel That Keeps Turning Until It Doesn't

The beginning almost always feels more original than it is.

That is not because the feeling is false. It may be deeply real. The person may matter in a way no one else has mattered before. The connection may carry its own texture, its own timing, its own private language. Something about the interaction may feel distinct enough that comparison feels almost disrespectful. This person is not like the others. This relationship is not following the old pattern. This time, something different is happening. Often, something different is happening. But something familiar is happening too.

Most relationships begin inside a recognizable emotional sequence. There is attention, activation, anticipation, and the steady narrowing of focus toward one person. The interaction gains significance. Small exchanges become memorable. Ordinary signals begin to carry meaning. A message, a glance, a shared joke, a late conversation, a remembered detail—all of it becomes part of an unfolding story.

At the beginning, the relationship has not yet become heavy. It has not yet been asked to carry accumulated disappointment, practical obligation, conflicting needs, family histories, financial pressure, fatigue, resentment, or the ordinary erosion that comes from being human in close proximity to another human being. It is not yet crowded with repair attempts that failed, conversations that ended too early, needs that were not named clearly, or fears that have been reinforced by repetition. The beginning is spacious. That spaciousness can feel like destiny.

Two people meet each other before the system has been stressed, and because there is little resistance, the relationship feels uniquely easy. It seems to move with its own intelligence. Each person feels more open, more available, more interested, perhaps even more generous than usual. The self that appears in the beginning often feels like the best self: less guarded, more alive, more willing to be known.

This is part of why early love is so persuasive. It does not only change how the other person is perceived. It changes how the self is perceived. A person may feel more patient, more hopeful, more emotionally capable, more ready for intimacy. The relationship seems to call forward a version of the self that had been waiting for the right conditions. But the early self is not the whole self. It is the self under favorable conditions (Sternberg, 1986; Hazan & Shaver, 1987).

This distinction is easy to miss because favorable conditions can produce real behavior. The attention is real. The generosity is real. The curiosity is real. The desire to understand and be understood is real. The mistake is not in believing those moments matter. They do. The mistake is in assuming they represent the full capacity of the relationship before the relationship has been exposed to pressure. The beginning tells the truth about what is possible under certain conditions. It does not yet tell the truth about what is sustainable under changing conditions.

This is where the cycle begins. Love accelerates before it stabilizes. The emotional system moves faster than the relational structure. Two people begin to feel as though they know something important about the relationship before enough time has passed to observe how it functions across difference, stress, boredom, conflict, and unmet expectation. The feeling creates confidence. Confidence creates investment. Investment creates momentum. Momentum is not the same as maturity. But it can feel like it.

In the acceleration phase, the relationship is rewarded often. There is frequent contact, emotional reinforcement, novelty, discovery, anticipation, and the pleasurable uncertainty of not yet knowing everything. The other person remains partly unknown, and that unknown space becomes filled with possibility. Each new detail seems to deepen the bond. Each moment of alignment becomes evidence. Each sign of mutual interest strengthens the story that something meaningful is unfolding.

Under these conditions, effort rarely feels like effort. Attention comes easily because attention is being rewarded. Communication is frequent because communication produces more connection. Flexibility is easier because the relationship has not yet asked for repeated sacrifice. Patience is easier because disappointment has not accumulated. Forgiveness is easier because the injuries are still small, if they exist at all. The system is being reinforced by pleasure (Skinner, 1953; Bandura, 1977).

This matters because a system reinforced by pleasure can feel stronger than it actually is. The early relationship may function well because the environment is designed, almost accidentally, to support functioning. Both people are motivated. Both are attentive. Both are invested in creating a positive experience. The relationship is operating with favorable inputs, and favorable inputs can conceal structural weakness.

A business can look successful during a period of high demand and low complexity. A team can seem cohesive when every project is exciting and every member is energized. A strategy can seem sound before the market changes. The test does not come when conditions support the system. The test comes when conditions shift and the system must rely on structure rather than momentum. The same is true in love.

Early momentum is powerful, but it is not proof that the relationship has learned how to hold. It only shows that the relationship knows how to move when movement is easy. Eventually, the movement changes.

This change is often subtle. It does not always arrive as conflict. More often, it arrives as a slowing. The relationship remains intact, but the automatic momentum begins to soften. Communication may still occur, but it does not always carry the same charge. Attention may still be present, but it becomes distributed among other responsibilities. The other person remains important, but the relationship is no longer protected from the rest of life. At first, this slowing can feel like loss.

The relationship no longer generates the same level of effortless reinforcement. A conversation that once would have lasted for hours now ends naturally after a few minutes. The response that once came quickly now waits behind work, fatigue, family obligations, or the simple mental noise of daily life. The gestures are still there, perhaps, but they are not as charged with novelty. The person is no longer being discovered in the same way. They are becoming familiar. Familiarity is not failure. But many people interpret it that way.

They compare the current relationship to its accelerated beginning and conclude that something essential has diminished. They begin to ask why the other person seems different, why the connection feels less intense, why communication requires more effort, why silence feels more noticeable, why the relationship feels less obvious than it once did. These questions are understandable, but they often carry the wrong assumption. They assume the beginning was the standard. The beginning was not the standard. It was the ignition.

No relationship can live indefinitely in ignition. It must eventually become something that can run without constant acceleration. It must develop habits, structure, rhythm, communication, repair, shared meaning, and the ability to remain connected without relying on novelty to do the work. This is where many relationships begin to falter, not because love has disappeared, but because the relationship has reached the point where feeling must become function. The wheel begins to turn.

In the first part of the cycle, the relationship is carried by activation. In the second, it begins to encounter exposure. The protected conditions of early connection give way to the ordinary conditions of life. Stress enters. Difference becomes more visible. Expectations become clearer, often because they are violated. The self that appeared so available in the beginning begins to meet the limits of energy, patience, and emotional capacity. This is where each person begins to see more of the other. Not necessarily worse versions. More complete versions.

The partner who seemed relaxed may become rigid under uncertainty. The partner who seemed expressive may become guarded when vulnerability carries risk. The partner who seemed independent may reveal difficulty with emotional dependence. The partner who seemed affectionate may struggle with consistency when overwhelmed. The partner who seemed easygoing may avoid necessary conflict. The partner who seemed confident may become defensive when feedback touches shame.

These revelations can feel disorienting because they appear to contradict the beginning. But often they do not contradict it. They complete it. The beginning showed who the person could be under conditions of attraction, novelty, and emotional reward. The next phase begins to show who the person becomes under conditions of stress, ambiguity, and expectation. Both are true. Only one is complete enough to build with.

This is where many people begin to feel betrayed by reality. They believe the relationship has changed into something less authentic, when in fact it may be becoming more accurate. The early stage was not false, but it was selective. It revealed certain capacities while leaving others untested. As the relationship develops, the untested areas begin to appear.

The first time this happens; it may be easy to dismiss. Everyone has difficult days. Everyone responds poorly at times. No relationship can be expected to maintain uninterrupted ease. These explanations are often reasonable, and they are sometimes correct. A single moment does not define the system. But repetition does (Gottman & Levenson, 1992; Schrodt et al., 2014).

The cycle becomes more visible when the same kinds of moments begin returning. A similar silence after a difficult topic. A similar defensiveness when a concern is raised. A similar urgency when uncertainty appears. A similar withdrawal when emotions become intense. A similar collapse into reassurance without change. A similar apology that repairs the mood but not the pattern. At this stage, the relationship begins to reveal whether it can learn from its own disruptions.

If it can, the cycle becomes developmental. The slowing of early intensity does not become decline. Exposure does not become collapse. Difference does not become threat. Instead, the relationship uses these moments to develop structure. Two people begin to clarify expectations, revise assumptions, understand triggers, create agreements, and build repair into the system. But if the relationship cannot learn, the cycle becomes repetitive. The same wheel turns.

The beginning gives way to exposure. Exposure produces strain. Strain activates old patterns. Old patterns create injury. Injury produces distance. Distance creates fear. Fear produces pursuit, withdrawal, control, appeasement, criticism, or silence. Those responses deepen the strain. Eventually, the relationship may recover enough to restore temporary closeness, but without learning, the underlying pattern remains unchanged. Then the wheel turns again.

This is one of the most painful aspects of unexamined love. The relationship may repeatedly move from closeness to strain and back again without ever understanding why the movement keeps occurring. After conflict, there may be relief. After distance, there may be reunion. After a difficult stretch, there may be a return of warmth that feels like proof the relationship is still strong. Sometimes it is proof of resilience. Sometimes it is only proof that the cycle has reset. The difference is whether anything was learned.

A reset returns the relationship to a prior emotional state without changing the pattern that produced the disruption. It feels good because the tension has decreased. The couple may feel close again. They may express love, recommit, apologize, promise to do better, or simply enjoy the relief of not being in conflict. But if the sequence remains unexamined, the relationship has not evolved. It has only returned to the top of the wheel. Learning is different (Baer et al., 1968; Baucom et al., 2011).

Learning changes the system. It identifies what happened, what was reinforced, what each person contributed, what assumption was operating, what repair requires, and what must be practiced differently next time. Learning does not merely restore closeness. It increases capacity.

The distinction between reset and learning is critical because many relationships mistake emotional recovery for relational growth. Feeling better is not the same as becoming better. Peace after conflict is not the same as repair. A return to affection is not the same as a new structure. The relationship may feel healed because the emotional charge has decreased, but the system may remain unchanged. This is why the wheel keeps turning.

The relationship encounters the same stresses with the same capacities and produces the same outcomes. Each repetition may feel slightly different because the topic changes, the timing changes, or the emotional intensity changes. But the underlying motion remains the same. What began as a cycle becomes a pattern of predictability.

At first, predictability can feel stabilizing. Even a painful pattern offers a kind of familiarity. Both people know their roles. One knows when to push. The other knows when to retreat. One knows when to apologize. The other knows when to soften. One knows how long the silence usually lasts. The other knows what gesture will restore the surface of connection. The relationship develops rituals of rupture and return. But rituals are not always repair. Some rituals merely make repetition livable.

A couple may become skilled at moving past tension without becoming skilled at understanding it. They may know how to return to normal without knowing what normal is costing them. They may develop tolerance for dysfunction because tolerance is easier than reconstruction. Over time, the cycle becomes part of the relationship's identity. This is just how we are. This is how we fight. This is how we come back together. This is what love feels like for us. That sentence can be dangerous. It may describe a relationship honestly. It may also protect the system from change.

The cycle gains power when it becomes normalized. What once felt concerning begins to feel expected. What once would have prompted reflection becomes part of the emotional routine. The couple stops asking why the wheel keeps turning and begins managing the discomfort of each rotation. This is how underdeveloped relationships can last for years.

Duration should not be confused with health. A relationship can continue because it is strong, but it can also continue because the cycle is familiar, the costs are gradual, and both people have adapted to patterns that do not ask enough of the system. The relationship survives, but survival is not the same as growth.

The cycle of love becomes especially difficult because it often contains enough genuine connection to keep hope alive. The relationship is not empty. There are moments of warmth, humor, attraction, care, tenderness, memory, and shared life. These moments are real, and because they are real, they complicate the decision to examine what is not working. It is easier to tolerate the wheel when parts of the ride still feel meaningful. This is why people stay confused.

If it were all bad, the pattern would be easier to name. If the person never cared, the conclusion would be simpler. If the relationship contained no love, no relief, no good days, no repair attempts, no evidence of possibility, the system would be less emotionally persuasive. But many relationships are not sustained by health alone. They are sustained by intermittent evidence of what could be. The good moments become proof that the relationship can work. The repeated pattern becomes proof that it has not learned how. Both truths can exist at the same time.

This is where maturity becomes necessary. Not the maturity of cynicism, where every good moment is dismissed as manipulation or illusion. Not the maturity of romantic denial, where every painful pattern is excused because love still appears between the cracks. The maturity required here is the ability to see the whole cycle, not just the moment that feels best or the moment that hurts most. The relationship must be understood across time.

Across time, the question becomes clearer. Does the relationship return to the same injuries with the same explanations? Does it require the same apologies without producing new behavior? Does closeness repeatedly depend on one person suppressing what they know needs to be addressed? Does peace arrive because the system has repaired, or because someone has stopped naming the problem?

These questions are not easy, but they are necessary because the cycle often hides inside emotion. When things are good, the pattern can seem less urgent. When things are bad, the pain can feel too immediate for reflection. The relationship swings between reassurance and alarm, leaving little room for sustained understanding.

Awareness begins when someone stops measuring the relationship only by its best moments or its worst moments and begins observing its movement. What happens after closeness? What happens after disappointment? What happens after conflict? What happens after apology? What happens after the promise to change? What happens when stress returns? The answers reveal the cycle.

This kind of observation can feel threatening because it removes the comfort of isolated interpretation. A beautiful weekend cannot be used to erase a recurring pattern. A painful argument cannot be used to define the entire relationship. The question is not which moment is the truth. The question is what pattern connects the moments.

The cycle may reveal that the relationship is maturing. It may show that each turn through difficulty produces more understanding, better repair, greater honesty, and more coordinated response. In that case, the wheel is not merely repeating. It is developing. The relationship is learning from its own movement.

But the cycle may also reveal that the relationship is stalled. It may show that each turn produces the same injury, the same explanation, the same temporary relief, and the same return to old conditions. In that case, the relationship is not moving forward. It is revolving. Revolving can be mistaken for progress because there is movement. But movement is not the same as growth.

A relationship grows when its capacity increases. It can hold more truth, respond with more flexibility, repair with more integrity, and adapt with more awareness. A relationship repeats when its emotional scenery changes but its structure remains the same. The couple feels as though they are going somewhere because the relationship is always in motion, but they keep arriving at the same place (Senge, 2006; Daks & Rogge, 2020).

The first time this becomes visible, it can feel devastating. It may reveal that years of effort have not produced the change either person believed was happening. It may reveal that what felt like repair was only relief. It may reveal that the relationship has been confusing endurance with evolution. But this recognition is also a point of possibility. A cycle cannot be changed while it remains invisible.

Once it is seen, the relationship has options it did not have before. The couple can begin identifying the points where the wheel turns. They can notice the early signs of acceleration, the assumptions that enter before conflict, the protective strategies that appear under stress, the unresolved injuries that give small moments disproportionate force. They can begin to ask what the cycle is trying to reveal rather than simply trying to survive another rotation. This is where the systems view becomes practical again.

The cycle is not magic. It is built from repeated interactions. It has triggers, reinforcements, expectations, and outcomes. It has points where one response makes another more likely. It has predictable emotional stations: activation, acceleration, strain, rupture, relief, and return. If those stations can be mapped, they can be interrupted. But interruption requires honesty about where the relationship actually is.

Many couples try to interrupt the cycle too late. They wait until the argument has escalated, until silence has lasted too long, until resentment has hardened, until one person has already begun emotionally leaving. By then, the pattern has gathered momentum. The wheel is already turning fast. The earlier the cycle is recognized, the more room there is to change it.

The early signs are often quiet. A familiar tightness when a topic comes up. A subtle shift in tone. The impulse to assume instead of ask. The urge to withdraw before anything has actually gone wrong. The first defensive sentence forming before the other person has finished speaking. The quick internal story that says, Here we go again. That moment matters.

It may seem small, but it is where the old pattern begins recruiting the present into the past. If nothing interrupts it, the system will likely continue toward the familiar outcome. If something different happens there, even something modest, the cycle is forced to adjust. A different question can interrupt it. A slower response can interrupt it. A direct statement of fear can interrupt it. A return after taking space can interrupt it. An acknowledgment of the pattern can interrupt it.

These interruptions do not automatically transform the relationship, but they weaken the inevitability of the wheel. They introduce a different possibility into a system that has learned to expect repetition. Over time, if repeated with consistency, they become the beginning of a new cycle. A learning cycle.

A learning cycle does not avoid difficulty. It moves through difficulty differently. It still begins with activation, because human beings will always be activated by closeness, difference, and unmet expectation. But instead of acceleration becoming automatic, the relationship begins to pause. Instead of strain becoming rupture, strain becomes information. Instead of apology becoming a return to the old pattern, repair becomes a change in the pattern. Instead of conflict proving that the relationship is broken, conflict reveals where the system needs development. This is the difference between a relationship that repeats and a relationship that learns. Repeating relationships use emotion to reset. Learning relationships use information to evolve.

Most relationships contain both tendencies. They repeat in some areas and learn in others. A couple may handle external stress beautifully but repeat the same cycle around vulnerability. They may coordinate well around practical decisions but struggle whenever one person feels emotionally unseen. They may repair quickly after minor conflicts but avoid deeper conversations that would require more structural change.

The goal is not to label the entire relationship as healthy or unhealthy based on one cycle. The goal is to identify which cycles govern the relationship most strongly and whether those cycles are capable of change. This requires patience, but not passivity.

Patience recognizes that patterns formed over time do not dissolve immediately. Passivity waits for the pattern to change without altering the conditions that sustain it. Patience remains engaged. It observes, interrupts, practices, and evaluates whether the system is actually learning.

This distinction matters because some people remain inside cycles for years in the name of patience. They believe love requires endurance, and sometimes it does. But endurance without learning can become participation in one's own depletion. A relationship that asks for patience must also show evidence of development. Otherwise, patience becomes another way the cycle protects itself. The wheel does not stop because people are tired. It stops because the system changes.

That change may come through shared effort. Both people begin seeing the pattern, naming it, taking responsibility, and practicing different responses. The relationship becomes more conscious. The wheel slows. What once felt inevitable begins to feel workable.

Or the change may come through one person's clarity. They may realize that the cycle is not changing because the relationship is not willing or able to learn. They may stop confusing temporary relief with progress. They may recognize that the good moments, while real, are not enough to sustain a system that repeatedly injures them without repair. In that case, stopping the cycle may mean stepping out of it. Both forms of change require seeing the pattern.

This is why the cycle of love is not simply a description of decline. It is a diagnostic movement. It shows where the relationship has matured and where it remains dependent on conditions that no longer exist. It reveals whether the couple can move from activation to awareness, from strain to learning, from rupture to repair, from repetition to growth.

The beginning of love often feels effortless because the wheel has not yet turned enough to reveal its mechanics. The middle becomes confusing because the wheel is turning but not yet understood. The later stages become defining because the couple must decide whether the cycle will remain unconscious or become part of the relationship's learning. There is no avoiding the wheel.

Every relationship moves. Every relationship changes conditions. Every relationship encounters the gap between what felt easy in the beginning and what must be built later. The question is not whether the cycle exists. The question is whether the people inside it can recognize what the cycle is teaching before it teaches the same lesson again. Love does not end only because feeling disappears. Sometimes love weakens because the same pattern keeps turning without becoming wiser. Sometimes it survives because the pattern is finally seen.

And sometimes it becomes stronger because two people stop trying to return to the beginning and begin building the structure the beginning never required.

CHAPTER SEVEN

THE SHIFT FROM ME TO US

Why Most Couples Never Become a Team

Most relationships begin with two people looking at each other.

They notice the chemistry, the ease, the curiosity, the feeling of being chosen and recognized. The relationship forms around attention. Each person becomes important to the other, and that importance begins to change the rhythm of ordinary life. Messages are anticipated. Plans are adjusted. Stories are shared. The presence of the other person becomes emotionally significant enough that the relationship begins to feel like its own world. But looking at each other is not the same as moving together.

This is one of the most consequential transitions in any relationship, and also one of the most frequently missed. Two people can be deeply connected, strongly attracted, emotionally invested, and sincerely committed, yet still not function as a team. They may love each other. They may want the relationship to last. They may even believe they are building a life together. But when stress enters, when decisions become complicated, when conflict exposes old patterns, or when life asks more from the relationship than affection can carry, they discover that they are still operating as separate individuals trying to manage the same situation from different internal worlds. They are together, but not yet integrated.

This distinction matters because many people assume that partnership happens automatically once commitment is present. If we choose each other, we must be a team. If we live together, we must be a team. If we love each other, we must naturally move in the same direction. The assumption feels reasonable because the language of relationship makes togetherness sound like structure.

Couple. Partner. Marriage. Family. These words imply a shared system, as though naming the bond creates the coordination required to sustain it. It does not. A relationship can have the title of partnership long before it has the functioning of one.

To become a team, two people have to do more than care about each other. They have to develop a shared way of responding to life. They have to learn how to carry stress without turning it into distance, how to make decisions without collapsing into control or avoidance, how to handle difference without making the relationship itself feel threatened. They have to become capable of asking not only, "What do I need?" but also, "What is happening between us, and what does the relationship need from both of us now?" That is a different level of maturity (Edmondson, 1999; Senge, 2006).

The movement from me to us is not the disappearance of individuality. It is not the surrender of identity, autonomy, preference, or personal responsibility. In fact, a healthy us requires two people who remain sufficiently whole as individuals. Fusion is not teamwork. Enmeshment is not intimacy. A relationship does not become stronger because one person absorbs the other or because both people pretend there is no longer any difference between them. The shift from me to us is not about losing the self. It is about bringing the self into coordination with another.

This is where many couples struggle. They think the alternative to self-protection is self-abandonment. They think that functioning as a team means agreeing, yielding, merging, or always prioritizing the relationship over the individual. But true partnership does not erase the individual. It asks the individual to become relationally aware. It asks each person to recognize that their choices, reactions, silence, timing, fears, and coping strategies do not remain private once they enter the shared system.

What you do to protect yourself may affect the relationship. What you avoid may become the other person's burden. What you refuse to name may become the atmosphere both of you have to breathe. What you manage alone may create distance in a place where closeness was needed. What you demand from the other person may be less about partnership than about asking them to regulate what you have not learned to hold.

The shift from me to us begins when both people understand that the relationship is not merely the place where individual needs compete. It is the system through which those needs must be understood, negotiated, and supported.

At the beginning, this is not always obvious. Early love often allows people to remain individually organized while feeling deeply connected. Each person continues to manage their own life, regulate their own stress, make their own assumptions, and interpret the relationship through their own framework. The connection may feel strong enough that these differences do not immediately matter. There is enough goodwill, novelty, and emotional reinforcement to keep the relationship moving. But eventually, life begins asking the relationship to function.

A decision has to be made. A disappointment has to be addressed. A family issue intrudes. Money becomes relevant. Work pressure changes availability. One person needs support in a way the other does not instinctively understand. A conflict arises that cannot be solved by affection alone. The relationship is no longer being sustained by the pleasure of connection. It is being tested by the demands of coordination. This is the moment when many couples discover they were never a team to begin with. They were two people who loved each other while managing themselves separately.

One person carries stress privately and calls it responsibility. The other feels excluded and calls it distance. One person seeks immediate discussion and calls it communication. The other feels overwhelmed and calls it pressure. One person needs reassurance and calls it connection. The other experiences the request as mistrust and calls it insecurity. Both may be trying to protect the relationship. Both may be trying to preserve something important. Yet their strategies collide because they are operating from individual logics rather than shared understanding.

Each person is asking, "How do I get through this?"

The relationship needs them to ask, "How do we get through this together?" That question sounds simple, but it reorganizes everything.

When people remain in a me orientation, the relationship becomes a place where individual reactions are defended rather than examined. Each person experiences their own internal state as the most urgent reality. If I feel pressured, you are pressuring me. If I feel ignored, you are ignoring me. If I feel unsafe, you are making me unsafe. If I feel criticized, you are attacking me. The feeling becomes the lens, and the lens becomes the relationship.

In an us orientation, the feeling still matters, but it is placed inside a wider field. I feel pressured, and I need to understand whether pressure is actually being applied or whether my system is reacting to the intensity of the moment. I feel ignored, and I need to communicate what I am experiencing without assuming your intention. I feel criticized, and I need to see whether feedback is being delivered poorly, whether I am hearing it through shame, or whether both are true. The emotional experience remains valid, but it is no longer allowed to become the only reality in the room. This is a major developmental shift.

It requires both people to loosen their loyalty to their own immediate interpretation long enough to become curious about the shared pattern. That does not mean denying one's experience. It means refusing to turn experience into a verdict before the relationship has had a chance to understand it.

Most couples do not fail because they lack feeling. They fail because they never build the practices that allow two emotional realities to become one shared conversation.

The private world remains private. Assumptions remain untested. Needs are hinted at rather than named. Fears are acted out rather than disclosed. Stress is managed individually until it spills into the relationship as irritation, silence, resentment, or withdrawal. The relationship becomes crowded with unspoken material, and both people begin reacting to an atmosphere that neither has fully acknowledged creating. This is how silence becomes distance.

Not all silence is harmful. Silence can be rest, regulation, peace, reflection, or comfort. Two people who trust each other can be quiet together without the quiet carrying threat. But in an unintegrated relationship, silence often becomes ambiguous. One person goes quiet to think, to recover, to avoid saying something poorly, or simply because they do not know what they feel yet. The other experiences the silence through their own model: distance, anger, rejection, punishment, indifference. Neither person may intend harm. The system still begins to change.

If the silence is not clarified, the other person fills in the meaning. If the meaning becomes painful, they may pursue, protest, withdraw, or harden. The person who went quiet may then feel accused, pressured, or misunderstood, which makes further silence more likely. What began as an individual coping strategy becomes a relational event. The relationship is now organizing around something neither person fully named. This is what happens when individual coping remains unshared. A person's internal strategy becomes the other person's external reality.

The same is true of independence. Independence can be healthy, necessary, and deeply attractive. A person who can manage their own life, regulate themselves, and remain grounded without constant reassurance brings strength into a relationship. But independence becomes relationally complicated when it is used to avoid mutuality. The person who prides themselves on handling things alone may not realize that their self-sufficiency creates exclusion. They may believe they are protecting the relationship by not burdening the other person. The other person may experience that same behavior as being shut out of the truth of their partner's life.

One says, "I did not want to worry you."

The other hears, "You did not trust me enough to include me." Again, the conflict is not simply about the behavior. It is about the meaning the behavior takes on inside the system.

A couple cannot become a team if one person's method of coping consistently prevents the other from participating in the reality of the relationship. Partnership requires access. Not access to every private thought, not the elimination of personal space, and not constant emotional disclosure. But enough access that the relationship is not forced to function on fragments. Enough access that the other person is not left guessing where they stand. Enough access that stress does not become a private burden that later appears as unexplained distance. To let someone in is not to make them responsible for everything you feel. It is to stop requiring the relationship to live outside the truth of what is affecting you.

This is a difficult lesson for people who have learned to survive by managing alone. For them, self-containment may feel like maturity. It may feel responsible, even loving. They may not understand why the other person feels distant from them when they are simply doing what they have always done: carrying the pressure, solving the problem, keeping the vulnerable parts private until they are manageable enough to share. But intimacy cannot deepen around only the edited version of the self. A partner cannot join you in a reality they are not allowed to see.

The opposite pattern can be equally difficult. Some people do not cope by withdrawing into privacy; they cope by pulling the other person into their emotional urgency. They do not merely want support. They need immediate relief. They ask the relationship to respond quickly, reassure completely, and resolve discomfort before it has been understood. Their fear becomes the organizing force of the interaction. This, too, prevents the shift from me to us.

It may look relational because it involves reaching. But reaching is not always partnership. Sometimes it is an individual regulation strategy that uses the other person as the stabilizing mechanism. The person may be saying, "I need us," but the underlying request is, "I need you to make this feeling stop." That is not shared functioning. It is emotional outsourcing.

The relationship can offer comfort, but it cannot become the sole container for every unregulated state. A healthy us does not mean one person becomes the nervous system for the other. It means both people learn how to bring their emotional experiences into the relationship in a way the relationship can actually hold. There is a difference between sharing fear and transferring fear.

Sharing fear says, "This is what is happening in me, and I want you to understand it." Transferring fear says, "This is what is happening in me, and now you must fix it or prove that it is not true." Sharing invites partnership. Transferring creates pressure. Sharing keeps responsibility connected to the self. Transferring relocates responsibility onto the other person. The shift from me to us requires both people to understand this difference.

It asks the withdrawing person to stop confusing privacy with strength. It asks the pursuing person to stop confusing urgency with intimacy. It asks the self-sufficient person to recognize that being loved means allowing another person to participate in more than the outcome. It asks the reassurance-seeking person to recognize that being loved does not mean making another person permanently responsible for emotional certainty. In each case, the movement is the same. The individual pattern must become available for shared understanding.

This is where team learning begins in the relational sense. In an effective team, members do not simply perform their individual roles side by side. They learn how their roles interact. They understand how one person's action affects another's capacity. They notice breakdowns in coordination. They develop shared language for what is happening. They adjust not only individually, but collectively. A relationship needs the same kind of learning (Senge, 2006; Edmondson, 1999).

Organizational research on psychological safety is useful here because learning requires more than intelligence. People have to believe that questions, concerns, mistakes, and unfinished thoughts can enter the system without humiliation or punishment. Translated into a relationship, psychological safety means that feedback can be brought forward before it becomes resentment, uncertainty can be named before it becomes distance, and repair can begin before self-protection becomes the only available strategy (Edmondson, 1999; Senge, 2006).

Not corporate language. Not mechanical process. Not a sterile conversion of intimacy into efficiency. But the underlying principle: two people who intend to move together must learn together. They must develop a way to notice when the system is drifting, when stress is being carried in isolation, when assumptions are replacing conversation, when repair is being delayed, and when the relationship is beginning to organize around protection instead of connection.

Without that shared learning, the couple remains dependent on individual insight. One person may understand their own pattern. The other may understand theirs. But unless those understandings become shared, the relationship does not necessarily change. Two privately self-aware people can still create a collectively unexamined relationship. The system requires shared awareness.

This is why the phrase "we need to communicate better" is both true and insufficient. Communication is not merely the exchange of information. Many couples talk often and still do not function as a team. They report events, explain positions, revisit disagreements, and express feelings, yet the relationship remains uncoordinated because the communication does not change the system. It does not clarify roles, align expectations, revise assumptions, or create a shared response to recurring patterns. Communication becomes useful when it helps the relationship organize itself more intelligently.

That requires a shift in purpose. The conversation is no longer only about being heard. It is about becoming understandable to each other in a way that changes what happens next. It is no longer only about expressing pain. It is about locating the pattern that keeps producing pain. It is no longer only about getting agreement. It is about building a shared model of what the relationship is facing. This is what most couples are missing when they say they cannot communicate. They may be able to speak. They have not yet learned how to think together.

Thinking together is not the same as agreeing. Agreement may come, or it may not. Thinking together means both people are willing to place the relationship in the center of the conversation rather than placing themselves in opposing positions. It means the problem is no longer simply mine or yours. It becomes ours, not because responsibility is equal in every instance, but because the relationship has to decide what to do with it.

This distinction is important. Moving from me to us does not mean every problem becomes equally shared. Some injuries are caused more directly by one person's behavior. Some patterns are maintained more heavily by one person's avoidance, reactivity, dishonesty, or lack of accountability. The language of us should never be used to dilute responsibility or make one person carry what belongs to the other. But even when responsibility is not equal, the relationship still requires a shared response.

If one person breaks trust, the person who caused the injury carries the primary responsibility for repair. But the relationship still has to create conditions in which repair can be understood, evaluated, and either accepted or rejected with clarity. If one person withdraws habitually, that person must take responsibility for the withdrawal. But the couple still needs to understand what happens in the system when withdrawal begins, how the other person responds, and what structure would make return possible. Us does not mean equal fault. It means shared reality.

A shared reality is one of the most important features of a resilient relationship. Without it, two people live in parallel interpretations. One believes the relationship is fine because conflict has decreased. The other believes the relationship is deteriorating because they have stopped bringing up what hurts. One believes they are giving space. The other believes they are being left alone. One believes they are being honest. The other believes honesty has become a cover for disregard.

When shared reality is absent, the relationship becomes difficult to repair because there is no common understanding of what is broken.

Each person argues from inside their own reality, trying to get the other to accept it. The conversation becomes a competition between versions of the relationship. The more each person defends their version, the less room there is to build a shared one. A team cannot function without shared reality.

It does not need perfect agreement, but it needs enough common ground to orient itself. It needs a way to say, "This is what we both recognize is happening, even if we experience it differently." That sentence is often the beginning of partnership. It allows two people to stop debating whether a problem exists and begin examining how it operates. The movement from me to us depends on that sentence.

It also depends on a willingness to see the relationship as something neither person owns alone. Many people enter conflict as though the relationship is the emotional property of their own experience. If I am hurt, the relationship is unsafe. If I am satisfied, the relationship is fine. If I feel close, we are close. If I feel distant, we are distant. The individual feeling becomes the measure of the whole system. But a relationship is larger than either person's current state.

One person may feel settled while the other is quietly losing trust. One may feel the issue has passed while the other is still carrying the injury. One may feel a conversation went well because they were able to explain themselves, while the other leaves feeling unseen because explanation replaced accountability. One person's relief is not always the same as relational repair. This is why teams need feedback.

A relationship without feedback becomes dependent on assumption. Each person guesses how the other is experiencing the system. They infer from mood, tone, behavior, routine, and history. Sometimes they are right. Often, they are not. Without feedback, small misalignments become larger ones. The relationship drifts, not because either person intended to move away, but because no one was checking the direction (Edmondson, 1999; Senge, 2006).

Feedback in a relationship does not have to be formal or constant. It is not a scorecard. It is the ongoing willingness to let the relationship tell the truth about how it is functioning. It is the ability to say, "This is starting to feel distant," before distance becomes resentment. "I think we are avoiding something," before avoidance becomes the norm. "I know we moved past that argument, but I do not think we repaired it," before unrepaired moments accumulate into distrust. This kind of feedback requires courage because it interrupts the comfort of pretending that silence means stability.

It also requires skill because feedback delivered without care can become criticism, and feedback received without maturity can become threat. A couple cannot become a team if every attempt to name the state of the relationship turns into blame or defense. The system needs a way to receive information about itself without collapsing.

This is where personal mastery and mental models return as essential foundations. A person who cannot regulate their reaction to feedback will struggle to participate in us. A person who interprets every concern as accusation will make shared learning nearly impossible. A person whose mental model says love should not require these conversations may experience the very act of checking in as evidence that something is wrong. But in a learning relationship, feedback is not evidence of failure. It is how the system stays alive.

A team that never reviews its performance does not remain strong by accident. It drifts. It repeats. It becomes dependent on habit. A relationship is no different. Without feedback, the couple may continue functioning, but functioning is not the same as improving. The routines may remain intact while emotional truth disappears beneath them. This is why the shift from me to us is not sentimental. It is structural.

It changes how stress is handled, how decisions are made, how repair occurs, how truth enters the relationship, and how both people understand their responsibility to the system. It asks each person to move beyond private survival and into shared stewardship.

Stewardship is a useful word here because it implies care without ownership. You do not own the relationship by yourself. You are entrusted with your part of it. Your choices affect its condition. Your neglect affects its condition. Your repair affects its condition. Your avoidance, honesty, tenderness, resentment, humor, criticism, patience, and courage all become part of what the relationship has to work with. To move from me to us is to become a steward of the shared system. That stewardship becomes most visible in moments of stress.

Stress is where many couples regress into separateness. Under pressure, old patterns return. One person focuses on tasks and becomes emotionally unavailable. Another focuses on emotion and feels unsupported by practical problem-solving. One becomes controlling because uncertainty feels dangerous. Another becomes passive because pressure feels overwhelming. One wants to talk immediately. Another needs time. One seeks closeness. Another seeks space. These differences do not automatically mean the relationship is incompatible. They mean the system needs coordination (Randall & Bodenmann, 2009; Falconier et al., 2015).

A team does not require identical responses. It requires an agreed way to work with differences. If one person needs time before discussing a painful issue, the relationship needs a structure for taking that time without abandoning the conversation. If one person needs reassurance during uncertainty, the relationship needs a way to offer care without making reassurance the only form of regulation. If one person becomes task-focused under stress, the relationship needs a way to include emotional information without shaming competence. If one person becomes emotionally expressive, the relationship needs a way to make that expression usable rather than overwhelming. The issue is not that people cope differently. The issue is whether their coping strategies can be integrated into a shared response.

Integration is not easy. It requires each person to translate their inner experience into language the relationship can use. "I need space" becomes more useful when it includes, "I am overwhelmed, not leaving, and I will come back to this conversation tonight." "I need reassurance" becomes more usable when it includes, "I am feeling scared, and I am working to stay grounded while asking for connection." "I am frustrated" becomes more relational when it includes, "I want to talk about this without turning it into an attack." The added structure matters. It turns individual coping into relational communication.

Without that structure, the other person is forced to interpret. Space may look like abandonment. Reassurance may feel like pressure. Frustration may land as criticism. The system begins responding not to what was intended, but to what was left undefined. This is why teams need shared language.

A relationship becomes more resilient when it develops words for its own patterns. Not clinical labels used as weapons, but language that helps both people recognize what is happening. "We are getting into the pursue-withdraw pattern." "I think we are both protecting ourselves instead of saying what is true." "This feels like one of those moments where we are talking about the schedule, but the real issue is feeling unsupported." "I am noticing that I want to defend myself instead of hearing you." Shared language slows the cycle.

It allows the relationship to name the pattern before the pattern fully takes over. It moves the couple from being inside the reaction to observing the reaction together. That shared observation is one of the first signs that two people are becoming a team. They are no longer only reacting as separate individuals. They are beginning to notice the system in real time.

This does not mean every moment becomes calm. In fact, the early attempts at shared language may be awkward. One person may use it too late, after the pattern has already escalated. Another may hear it as analysis rather than care. Both may struggle to trust the shift because the old cycle is familiar and the new way of engaging feels uncertain. That is expected.

A team is not built by understanding the concept once. It is built through repeated attempts to coordinate under real conditions. The couple has to practice naming the pattern, repairing after missteps, and returning to shared purpose after falling into old roles. They have to learn that the goal is not to avoid every breakdown, but to become increasingly capable of recognizing and repairing breakdowns when they occur (Argyris & Schön, 1978; Senge, 2006).

This is where many couples become discouraged. They think that because they understand the pattern, they should no longer fall into it. But understanding arrives before embodiment. The mind may see what the relationship is doing long before the nervous system knows how to do something different. Old patterns remain accessible because they have been practiced. New patterns require repetition before they feel natural. Teamwork is built through practice, not insight alone.

At first, practice may look unimpressive. A conversation still becomes tense, but one person notices sooner. A withdrawal still happens, but the person returns more reliably. A defensive response still appears, but it is named and repaired. A need is still expressed imperfectly, but it is followed by clarification rather than escalation. These small differences may not feel dramatic enough to count as change, but they are exactly how systems begin to shift. A relationship does not become a team in one breakthrough. It becomes a team when repeated moments begin to show that the relationship can rely on a different pattern.

Reliability matters because us cannot be built on occasional maturity. A person who shows up differently only when the relationship is at risk teaches the system that change requires crisis. A person who communicates well only after distance has become painful teaches the system that clarity arrives late. A person who repairs only when consequences are imminent teaches the system that accountability depends on pressure. For teamwork to become real, the new pattern has to appear when the stakes are ordinary.

The relationship has to experience care in the small moments, not only the dramatic ones. It has to experience return after minor withdrawal, accountability after small impact, clarification after subtle misunderstanding, and shared attention before drift becomes rupture. These ordinary repetitions create the confidence that the system can hold. This is where the relationship begins to feel different.

Not because it is constantly intense, but because it becomes more dependable. The other person is no longer merely someone you love. They become someone with whom you can face reality. You can bring the difficult thing and trust that the system will not immediately collapse into blame, avoidance, or performance. You can disagree without assuming disconnection. You can name distance without creating more distance. You can expose a fear without making it the other person's prison. The relationship becomes less fragile because it is no longer dependent on everything going well. It has learned how to function when things do not.

This is the point at which the idea of partnership becomes more than a title. The relationship begins to have a shared mind. Not because the two people think identically, but because they have developed a shared way of making sense of what happens between them. They have a language for their patterns. They have a way to bring feedback into the system. They have enough personal mastery to remain present, enough humility to question their models, and enough shared vision to remember what they are trying to build. Without shared vision, even teamwork can become reactive.

Two people may learn to manage conflict more effectively and still lack a clear sense of direction. They may become better at getting through difficult moments without knowing what the relationship is ultimately organized around. The shift from me to us requires not only shared coping, but shared purpose.

Purpose does not have to be grand. It does not need to sound poetic or abstract. In a relationship, shared purpose may be as simple and profound as the commitment to build a home where both people can tell the truth, repair harm, grow without being punished for changing, and remain connected without losing themselves. It may be the commitment to raise children in an environment where conflict is not hidden but handled with respect. It may be the commitment to become a place of stability in a world that often feels unstable. It may be the commitment to keep choosing the relationship consciously rather than relying on inertia. Purpose gives the team direction.

Without it, couples often default to maintenance. They try to keep the relationship going, keep conflict down, keep routines functioning, keep the peace. Maintenance is necessary, but it is not enough. A relationship that only maintains may slowly lose the reason it is being maintained. It remains intact but not alive. It continues but does not deepen. Shared purpose turns the relationship toward growth.

It allows two people to ask whether their current patterns serve what they are trying to build. Does the way we handle stress support the kind of partnership we say we want? Does the way we communicate create the emotional climate we want to live in? Does the way we repair strengthen trust, or merely end conflict?

Does the way we protect ourselves prevent us from becoming the team we intended to be? These questions are not easy. But they are the questions that move a relationship from coexistence to partnership.

Coexistence can look stable. Two people share space, responsibilities, routines, and affection. They may function well enough for a long time. But coexistence often relies on parallel management. Each person handles their own world, and the relationship exists in the overlap. That may be sufficient for a season. It may even feel peaceful. But when life becomes more demanding, the limits of coexistence become clear. Partnership requires more.

It requires the relationship to become a place where life is processed, not merely reported. It requires decisions to be made with awareness of the system, not only individual preference. It requires stress to be shared in ways that do not overwhelm or exclude. It requires both people to understand that independence and interdependence are not enemies. The strongest relationships are not made of two people who need nothing from each other, nor two people who need everything from each other. They are made of two people who can stand on their own and still know how to stand together. That balance is difficult because human beings often lean toward the pattern they know best.

Those who fear dependence may overvalue autonomy. Those who fear abandonment may overvalue closeness. Those who fear conflict may overvalue peace. Those who fear invisibility may overvalue expression. In each case, the individual strategy may make sense, but the relationship needs integration. Autonomy must learn how to remain connected. Closeness must learn how to respect space. Peace must learn how to include truth. Expression must learn how to consider impact. This is the work of us. It is not a sentimental state. It is a disciplined way of relating.

The discipline lies in remembering the relationship when the self is activated. When anger wants to win, us remembers impact. When fear wants control, us remembers trust. When shame wants defense, us remembers accountability. When overwhelm wants disappearance, us remembers return. When longing wants certainty, us remembers that reassurance is meaningful but cannot replace self-regulation. This remembering is not automatic. It has to be practiced until it becomes part of the system.

In the beginning, each person may need to remind themselves deliberately. What am I doing to the system right now? Am I trying to be understood, or am I trying to win? Am I asking for closeness, or am I demanding relief? Am I taking space, or am I abandoning the process? Am I protecting myself in a way that makes partnership impossible?

These questions are not meant to create self-surveillance. They are meant to restore choice. In the absence of these questions, old patterns make decisions on behalf of the relationship. With them, the person has a chance to enter the system differently. A couple becomes a team when both people practice that kind of entry.

They begin to bring themselves into the relationship with more awareness. They become less careless with the shared space. They recognize that the relationship has a climate, and that climate is affected by repeated behavior. They stop assuming the relationship can absorb every unexamined reaction without consequence. They begin to understand that love is not only expressed in affection, but in the willingness to protect the system from one's own worst habits. That protection is not repression. It is responsibility.

It is the person who says, "I am angry, but I will not use contempt." It is the person who says, "I need space, but I will return." It is the person who says, "I feel scared, but I will not turn fear into accusation." It is the person who says, "I disagree, but I will not make you my opponent." It is the person who says, "I am ashamed, but I will not use defensiveness to escape accountability." These are the small vows of partnership.

They matter more than many of the vows people make publicly because they are practiced in private, under pressure, when the relationship is most vulnerable to old patterns.

The shift from me to us does not happen because two people stop having individual needs. It happens because individual needs become part of a shared system of care. One person's need for space is held alongside the other's need for reassurance. One person's need for directness is held alongside the other's need for gentleness. One person's need for autonomy is held alongside the other's need for inclusion. The relationship becomes the place where these needs are not simply traded or fought over, but understood and organized. That organization is what makes love sustainable.

Without it, the relationship becomes a recurring negotiation between competing protections. With it, the relationship becomes a coordinated response to the complexity of being two different people trying to build one life.

This is not easy, and it is not always symmetrical. There will be seasons when one person has more capacity than the other. Seasons when stress is unevenly distributed. Seasons when one person needs more support, more patience, more steadiness. A team does not require perfect equality in every moment. But it does require a larger pattern of mutuality. If one person is always the container, always the regulator, always the one who adapts, always the one who returns, always the one who carries the shared system, the relationship is not functioning as a team. It is functioning around an imbalance. Us cannot be built on one person's disappearance.

That is why the shift must include both people. One person can begin it. One person can model it. One person can change their own participation and create new possibilities in the system. But one person cannot become us alone. If the relationship is to become a team, both people must eventually participate in shared awareness, shared responsibility, and shared repair.

When that participation happens, the emotional experience of the relationship changes in a way that is difficult to describe but unmistakable to those who have felt it. It feels like not being alone in the problem.

Not because the other person fixes everything. Not because they always understand immediately. Not because conflict disappears. It feels different because the relationship no longer leaves each person isolated inside their own interpretation. There is a sense that even when something is hard, both people are facing in the same direction. The issue may still hurt, but it does not automatically become a battle over whose pain matters more. The stress may still be real, but it does not have to become distance. The conflict may still need work, but it does not have to threaten the entire bond. The relationship becomes a place where difficulty can be brought. That is when partnership begins to feel real.

Not in the fantasy of being perfectly understood, but in the experience of being joined in the work of understanding. Not in the absence of fear, but in the presence of someone willing to help build a system where fear does not run everything. Not in the performance of unity, but in the repeated evidence that both people are willing to protect the shared life they are creating. This is the relationship becoming real in a deeper sense.

The early relationship may have been real in feeling. The connection was real. The hope was real. The attraction and affection were real. But this stage asks for a different kind of reality. It asks whether the relationship can become real in function. Can it hold stress? Can it tell the truth? Can it adapt? Can it repair? Can it become a place where two people are not merely emotionally attached, but relationally coordinated? The answer to those questions determines what love becomes over time.

If the shift from me to us never happens, the relationship may continue, but it will remain vulnerable to the limits of individual coping. Each person will keep managing their own experience while hoping the other somehow understands. The system will keep producing distance where coordination was needed. Love may still be present, but it will be forced to operate through a structure too narrow to support it. If the shift does happen, the relationship begins to enter a different stage of development.

The question changes from "Do you love me?" to "Can we build something that knows how to hold us both?" It changes from "Are my needs being met?" to "How do our needs become part of a shared life?" It changes from "Who caused this?" to "What is happening between us, and what does this moment require from each of us?" That is the movement from me to us. It is not the end of individuality. It is the beginning of partnership.

And once a relationship begins to move in that direction, love is no longer just something two people feel for each other. It becomes something they are learning how to do together.

CHAPTER EIGHT

WHAT LOVE IS ACTUALLY MADE OF

Beyond Feeling, Beyond Fantasy

By the time a relationship reaches the point where two people are trying to become a team, the old language of love often begins to feel too small.

It is not that the language is wrong. People still want affection, closeness, trust, commitment, attraction, tenderness, and a sense of being chosen. These are not superficial desires. They are part of what makes love worth wanting in the first place. A relationship without warmth becomes an arrangement. A relationship without desire becomes fragile in a different way. A relationship without commitment struggles to survive inconvenience, disappointment, and time. But as love matures, the question changes. It is no longer enough to ask whether love is present. The more important question becomes what kind of love has been built.

This question is harder to answer because love is often treated as though it is one thing. People speak of being in love, falling out of love, finding love, losing love, proving love, choosing love, and fighting for love, as though the word itself carries a complete understanding. But love is not a single substance. It is not one feeling, one decision, one bond, one promise, or one form of attachment. It is a living combination of emotional connection, behavioral consistency, psychological safety, shared meaning, desire, trust, commitment, and adaptive capacity. When people do not understand this, they mistake one part of love for the whole.

They feel passion and assume the relationship has depth. They feel comfort and assume the relationship has safety. They feel loyalty and assume the relationship has intimacy. They make a commitment and assume the relationship has structure. They share history and assume the relationship has resilience. Each assumption contains a partial truth, which is why it is so convincing. But partial truths become dangerous when they are allowed to stand in for the whole. A relationship can have passion and still be unstable. It can have commitment and still be lonely. It can have intimacy and still lack direction. It can have loyalty and still avoid truth. It can have history and still fail to learn.

This is why the question of what love is actually made of matters. Without that question, people tend to evaluate the relationship by whichever part of love is most emotionally available to them in the moment. When passion is high, they believe the relationship is strong. When conflict decreases, they believe the relationship is improving. When commitment remains, they believe love is intact. When closeness returns after distance, they believe the problem has been resolved. Sometimes they are right. Often, they are only seeing one component.

A mature understanding of love requires the ability to hold several truths at once. Love can be deeply felt and still poorly structured. It can be sincere and still underdeveloped. It can be loyal and still unskilled. It can be emotionally meaningful and still unable to sustain the conditions placed upon it. None of this makes love false. It makes love insufficiently understood. This is the point where fantasy begins to fall away.

Fantasy does not always look childish. It does not always appear as unrealistic romance or dramatic longing. Sometimes fantasy appears as an unexamined belief that one part of love should compensate for the absence of another. If the attraction is strong enough, the relationship should survive the instability. If the commitment is sincere enough, loneliness should be tolerable. If the history is long enough, the lack of repair should matter less. If the intention is good enough, the repeated impact should be forgiven. Fantasy asks one part of love to do the work of the entire system. Reality eventually refuses.

The refusal may appear slowly. A couple may remain committed but begin to feel emotionally unknown. They may share a home, responsibilities, routines, and memories, yet feel less able to speak honestly than they were years before. They may still love each other in the sense of caring deeply, but the relationship no longer feels alive. The bond remains, but the intimacy has thinned.

Another couple may have intensity, desire, and emotional charge, but little stability. Their connection feels powerful, but the relationship cannot hold conflict without becoming chaotic. They mistake the return after rupture for proof of depth, when the pattern may actually reveal a system that confuses instability with aliveness. Passion keeps pulling them back together, but nothing structural changes enough to make the relationship safer.

Another couple may have steadiness and loyalty, but little adaptation. They do what they promised to do. They stay. They provide. They continue. But they do not learn. They do not revise the patterns that have stopped serving them. They do not ask whether the relationship they are preserving is still capable of holding the people they have become. Commitment remains, but growth has stalled. These are not uncommon failures. They are failures of composition. Something important is present. Something else is missing.

To understand love as a system, we have to stop asking only whether a relationship contains love and begin asking how its components interact. Passion, intimacy, and commitment are often treated as the major elements of romantic love, and they do matter. Passion brings energy, attraction, desire, and the sense that the relationship has emotional and physical vitality. Intimacy brings closeness, knowledge, vulnerability, and the experience of being seen. Commitment brings continuity, direction, and the decision to remain engaged beyond the fluctuations of feeling (Sternberg, 1986).

Relationship science supports this broader composition of love. Sternberg's triangular model gives language to passion, intimacy, and commitment, while attachment research shows how security, responsiveness, and emotional accessibility shape the way romantic bonds function under stress. Couple-therapy research adds another layer: love becomes more durable when partners can regulate emotion, respond to vulnerability, and repair attachment injuries rather than merely return to the appearance of closeness (Sternberg, 1986; Hazan & Shaver, 1987; Wiebe & Johnson, 2016; Beasley & Ager, 2019).

But even these elements do not exist independently. They affect one another. Passion without safety can become volatility. Intimacy without desire can become companionship without aliveness. Commitment without emotional presence can become endurance without connection. Desire can deepen intimacy, but it can also mask incompatibility. Commitment can stabilize love, but it can also preserve patterns that should be confronted. Intimacy can create closeness, but if the relationship cannot hold difference, that closeness may collapse under stress. The relationship is not defined by whether each element exists in some abstract sense. It is defined by how those elements function together.

Passion is perhaps the easiest to recognize and the easiest to misunderstand. It announces itself with force. It gives the relationship energy. It makes attention feel effortless, contact feel significant, and possibility feel immediate. Passion is not shallow simply because it is physical or emotional. It can be a powerful form of aliveness. It can open people to parts of themselves that had grown dormant. It can bring play, vitality, longing, and the sense that the relationship matters not only in practical terms but in the body. The problem is not passion. The problem is asking passion to prove what it cannot prove.

Passion cannot prove that two people can repair harm. It cannot prove they share values. It cannot prove they can tell the truth under pressure, respect boundaries, manage disappointment, or build a life together. Passion can create urgency, but urgency is not the same as readiness. It can make the relationship feel important, but importance is not the same as structure.

When passion is treated as evidence of depth, people may ignore the places where the relationship is underdeveloped. They may tolerate inconsistency because the reunion feels powerful. They may explain away conflict because the intensity of connection afterward feels meaningful. They may confuse emotional highs and lows with proof that the relationship is profound, when sometimes the system is simply unstable.

This does not mean calm is always healthier than intensity. A passionless relationship may be stable but emotionally vacant. The goal is not to eliminate intensity. The goal is to understand what intensity is doing inside the system. Is it bringing vitality to a relationship that also has safety, honesty, and repair? Or is it compensating for the absence of those things? Passion becomes healthier when it is held by structure.

Without structure, it can become a force that keeps the relationship moving without helping it mature. With structure, it becomes part of the relationship's vitality rather than its primary source of stability.

Intimacy is more subtle. It is often mistaken for disclosure, familiarity, or time spent together. Two people may know many details about each other and still lack intimacy. They may share routines, histories, family stories, preferences, and private jokes, yet avoid the truths that would make the relationship more honest. They may be close in proximity but distant in reality. Intimacy is not merely knowing information. It is the experience of being known accurately and received with enough care that truth remains possible.

This makes intimacy more demanding than many people expect. It requires more than emotional expression. It requires listening that does not immediately correct, dismiss, or defend. It requires the ability to reveal without performing, to hear without collapsing, and to respond to vulnerability without making it unsafe. It requires both people to make room for the parts of the other that are inconvenient to their preferred story of the relationship. Many relationships lose intimacy not because people stop talking, but because they stop telling the truth (Hazan & Shaver, 1987; Wiebe & Johnson, 2016).

The truth may not disappear all at once. It may become edited. One person stops naming disappointment because the other becomes defensive. The other stops admitting uncertainty because it triggers panic. Someone stops sharing desire because rejection has become too painful. Someone stops asking hard questions because every answer becomes an argument. The relationship continues, but a narrower version of each person is allowed to enter it. Over time, this narrowing is felt as distance.

The couple may still function. They may still care about each other. They may still say the right things. But something essential has been lost. The relationship no longer has access to the full truth of the people inside it. This is the quiet loss of intimacy.

It does not always look like disconnection. Sometimes it looks like peace. The couple stops fighting because they have stopped bringing forward the material that would create conflict. They appear stable because the system has learned to avoid what it cannot hold. But avoidance is not intimacy. Silence is not safety. A relationship that can only remain calm by excluding truth is not emotionally secure. It is managed. Real intimacy requires a system that can survive truth.

That truth includes needs, limits, disappointments, fears, desires, changes, and the ways each person has been affected by the other. It includes the truth that one person may feel lonely even inside commitment. It includes the truth that attraction may need attention rather than assumption. It includes the truth that old patterns are still operating, that apologies have not fully repaired, that love is present but something in the system is not working. A relationship that cannot hear these truths may preserve the appearance of love while weakening its substance.

Commitment is the third element people often mistake for the whole. Commitment matters enormously. It is one of the ways love survives the instability of emotion. It allows a relationship to continue through seasons when feeling is less dramatic, when stress is high, when life is demanding, when the other person is not easy to love in the immediate sense. Commitment provides continuity. It says the relationship is not abandoned every time discomfort appears. Without commitment, love remains vulnerable to mood. But commitment alone is not enough.

A person can stay and still not show up. They can remain in the relationship while withholding emotional presence, accountability, curiosity, or repair. They can fulfill obligations while avoiding intimacy. They can point to duration as proof of love while the relationship slowly loses the capacity to grow. Commitment without connection becomes a structure without warmth. Commitment without repair becomes a container for resentment. Commitment without adaptation becomes endurance.

This is one of the most painful forms of relational confusion because commitment is often morally valued. People admire staying. They respect loyalty. They see perseverance as evidence of character, and often it is. But staying is not always the same as loving well. Loyalty to the relationship must include loyalty to the health of the relationship, not merely loyalty to its continuation. A relationship can be preserved in a form that damages both people.

That is not mature commitment. It is attachment to the structure without enough attention to what the structure is becoming.

Healthy commitment is active. It does not simply remain. It participates. It asks what the relationship needs in order to continue with integrity. It supports repair, not avoidance. It protects the bond, but not at the expense of truth. It is willing to adapt because it understands that the point is not merely to keep the relationship alive, but to keep it capable of supporting life. This is where love becomes more complex than the usual categories allow.

Passion, intimacy, and commitment matter, but the relationship also needs psychological safety. It needs trust built through repeated behavior. It needs shared meaning, not merely shared history. It needs the ability to adapt when conditions change. It needs a way to use feedback without collapsing into blame. It needs enough personal mastery that both people can remain present when the system becomes stressful. It needs enough humility to revise mental models that no longer serve the relationship. In other words, love is not only an emotional bond. It is a functioning system of care.

Care is often misunderstood as intention. A person may say, "I care about you," and mean it sincerely. But inside a relationship, care must become visible through pattern. It must show up in what is noticed, what is protected, what is repaired, what is repeated, and what is changed when the current pattern harms the relationship. Care that never becomes behavior leaves the system unsupported.

A person may care deeply and still be careless with impact. They may care deeply and still avoid necessary conversations. They may care deeply and still refuse to examine the way their defensiveness blocks repair. They may care deeply and still create instability because they do not know how to translate care into consistent relational action.

This distinction is difficult because people often experience care as internal truth. They know what they feel. They know their intention. They know the private tenderness or loyalty they carry. But the relationship does not live only with internal truth. It lives with what becomes enacted. Love must be expressed in a form the relationship can use.

That form includes behavior, timing, tone, consistency, repair, and the willingness to learn. It includes knowing when affection is needed and when accountability is needed more. It includes understanding that reassurance offered without change can become hollow. It includes recognizing that apologies are not emotional resets but commitments to alter the pattern that made the apology necessary. This is why trust becomes central.

Trust is not simply belief in another person's goodness. It is confidence in the pattern of their behavior. You trust someone when the relationship has repeatedly shown you that certain things can be relied upon. You trust that honesty will be met with seriousness. You trust that conflict will not become contempt. You trust that taking space will not become disappearance. You trust that repair will involve change, not only regret. You trust that the other person's care has enough structure to survive stress. Trust is built through evidence. It is weakened through evidence as well (Gottman & Levenson, 1992; Baucom et al., 2011).

This is why good intentions cannot restore trust by themselves. If the system has learned inconsistency, it will not become secure through verbal reassurance alone. If the system has learned that vulnerability leads to dismissal, it will not become open because one person insists, they are safe. If the system has learned that accountability is avoided, it will not trust accountability until accountability becomes repeated behavior. Trust is the relationship's memory of what has happened often enough to become expected.

That memory cannot be argued away. It has to be updated through experience. This is why repair takes time, and why a single sincere moment may not be enough to change the emotional reality of the relationship. The person offering repair may feel the intensity of their intention. The person receiving repair is responding to the history of the pattern. Both experiences may be real. The relationship will change only when the pattern changes consistently enough for trust to reorganize.

Psychological safety grows from that kind of trust. It is the sense that the relationship can hold truth, difference, discomfort, and vulnerability without turning them into punishment, withdrawal, contempt, or chaos. Safety does not mean constant comfort. In fact, some of the most important conversations in a healthy relationship are uncomfortable. Safety means discomfort can be entered without the system becoming dangerous to the people inside it (Edmondson, 1999; Johnson, 2020).

A psychologically safe relationship can hear, "I am hurt," without immediately making the hurt an attack. It can hear, "I need something different," without making the need a threat. It can hear, "This pattern is not working," without turning the conversation into a battle for self-protection. It can make room for feedback because feedback is not automatically equated with rejection. Without safety, love becomes guarded.

People may still love each other, but they begin protecting themselves from the relationship. They withhold, manage, soften, test, monitor, perform, or retreat. The relationship becomes less a place of mutual development and more a place of strategic self-protection. Over time, the emotional cost rises. The system may continue, but intimacy becomes increasingly expensive. This is why love must include more than affection.

Affection may soften the relationship, but safety determines whether truth can enter it. Desire may energize the relationship, but trust determines whether vulnerability can survive. Commitment may keep the relationship intact, but adaptation determines whether it can grow. Adaptation is one of the least romantic and most necessary components of love.

Every relationship changes because the people inside it change. Life changes. Bodies change. Work changes. Family structures change. Needs change. Values become clearer. Old coping strategies stop working. New pressures arrive. A relationship that cannot adapt begins to rely on an outdated version of itself.

Many couples suffer because they are trying to preserve a relationship built for earlier conditions. The patterns that worked in the beginning no longer fit the life they are living. The way they communicated before children, illness, career shifts, financial strain, grief, or aging may not support them now. The forms of affection that once felt sufficient may need to evolve. The assumptions that once went unchallenged may need to be renegotiated. Love that cannot adapt becomes nostalgia.

It keeps reaching backward for a version of the relationship that belonged to another stage. It asks the present to resemble the past rather than asking the relationship to become capable of the present. This creates grief, frustration, and often blame. One person may feel the other has changed. The other may feel they are being asked to remain the same in conditions that no longer allow it. The truth is that change is not the enemy of love. Unprocessed change is.

A relationship that expects change can respond to it. It can ask what needs to be revised, what needs to be mourned, what needs to be protected, and what needs to be built differently. It does not assume that every shift in feeling means decline. It understands that love must be restructured across seasons if it is going to remain alive.

This is where shared meaning becomes important. A relationship is not sustained by mechanics alone. It needs a reason to continue building. It needs a sense of what the relationship is for, what kind of life it is trying to support, what values it is organized around, and what both people are choosing beyond habit. Shared meaning gives the system direction (Senge, 2006; Gottman & Silver, 2015).

Without shared meaning, couples may become efficient but emotionally thin. They may handle tasks, manage schedules, resolve conflicts, and maintain routines, yet still feel that something central is missing. The relationship functions, but it does not nourish. It survives, but it does not orient the lives inside it toward anything larger than maintenance.

Shared meaning is not necessarily dramatic. It may be found in building a home where truth is possible. It may be found in raising children with more emotional awareness than either person received. It may be found in creating stability after lives shaped by chaos. It may be found in friendship, service, creativity, faith, adventure, healing, or the simple dignity of being known over time. But it must be shared enough to matter.

If one person believes the relationship is primarily a place of emotional intimacy and the other sees it primarily as a practical partnership, the system will eventually feel the difference. If one person values growth and the other values comfort above all else, the system will feel the difference. If one person wants the relationship to become more conscious while the other wants it to remain familiar, the system will feel the difference. Love does not require identical purpose. It requires enough shared meaning to coordinate difference.

This is why two people can have many components of love and still feel that something is not working. Passion may be present. Intimacy may exist in certain areas. Commitment may be strong. Trust may be partial. Safety may be inconsistent. Adaptation may be low. Shared meaning may be assumed rather than clarified. The relationship contains love, but its composition is uneven. Uneven composition is not always fatal. It is information.

It tells the couple where the system is underdeveloped. It reveals which component has been overused and which has been neglected. It shows whether passion is covering a lack of safety, whether commitment is covering a lack of intimacy, whether shared history is covering a lack of adaptation, whether affection is covering a lack of repair.

This is a more useful way to understand relational distress than asking whether love is still there. Love may be there. The question is whether the form of love present is capable of supporting the relationship under its current conditions. That question brings maturity to the center.

An immature view of love asks, "Do I feel it?"

A more mature view asks, "What does this love require in order to function?" An immature view asks, "Is the connection strong?"

A more mature view asks, "Can this connection survive truth, difference, stress, and repair?" An immature view asks, "Are we committed?"

A more mature view asks, "What are we committed to building, and are our patterns aligned with that commitment?"

These questions do not make love colder. They make it more accountable. They prevent the relationship from hiding behind the emotional legitimacy of one component while neglecting the rest of the system. This matters because love often fails in the gap between what people feel and what they practice.

A person may feel devoted but practice avoidance. They may feel protective but practice control. They may feel remorse but practice defensiveness. They may feel desire but practice inconsistency. They may feel loyalty but practice silence in the face of what needs to be addressed. The relationship is shaped by the practice.

That does not mean feeling is irrelevant. Feeling gives love its emotional life. But practice gives love its relational form. Without practice, feeling remains vulnerable to mood, memory, and interpretation. Without feeling, practice can become mechanical. A mature relationship needs both. It needs the warmth of love and the structure of love. It needs tenderness and truth. It needs desire and steadiness. It needs commitment and adaptation. It needs a form of love that can be lived.

This is why love, understood as a system, becomes more demanding than fantasy but also more hopeful. Fantasy offers the hope that the right feeling will make the work unnecessary. Systems love offers a different hope: that the work, when understood and shared, can make love more durable than feeling alone could ever make it.

This kind of love is not built in abstraction. It appears in ordinary moments. It appears when someone tells the truth gently instead of avoiding it. It appears when someone receives feedback without immediately defending. It appears when someone returns after needing space. It appears when apology becomes changed behavior. It appears when desire is protected through attention rather than assumed as a permanent condition. It appears when commitment is expressed not only by staying, but by continuing to participate in the relationship's development. It appears when two people stop asking love to remain effortless and begin asking how to make it more capable.

Capability is not a word people often associate with love, but it belongs here. A relationship has capacities. It can be more or less capable of handling conflict, stress, grief, change, intimacy, disappointment, difference, and growth. Love may be present, but if the relationship lacks these capacities, love will be placed under strain it cannot survive indefinitely.

A capable relationship can be honest without becoming cruel. It can be close without becoming fused. It can be independent without becoming distant. It can be committed without becoming stagnant. It can be passionate without becoming unstable. It can be peaceful without becoming avoidant. It can change without interpreting every change as loss. This is what love is actually made of when fantasy is no longer carrying the story. It is made of feeling, but not feeling alone.

It is made of choice, but not choice alone. It is made of behavior repeated often enough to become trust. It is made of truth held carefully enough to become intimacy. It is made of repair practiced consistently enough to become safety. It is made of desire protected intentionally enough to remain alive. It is made of commitment active enough to support growth. It is made of meaning shared clearly enough to guide direction. And it is made of a system flexible enough to learn (Daks & Rogge, 2020; Barraca et al., 2025).

This is not a lesser view of love. It is a fuller one. It honors the emotional power of love without asking that power to do what only structure can do. It allows passion to matter without allowing passion to excuse instability. It allows commitment to matter without allowing commitment to preserve disconnection. It allows intimacy to matter without reducing intimacy to disclosure alone. It allows trust, safety, meaning, adaptation, and repair to become visible as parts of love rather than optional additions to it. Once this view is understood, certain questions become unavoidable. What part of love has this relationship relied on most heavily? What part has been neglected? Where has feeling been asked to replace structure? Where has commitment been asked to replace intimacy? Where has affection been asked to replace repair? Where has history been asked to replace growth?

The answers may be uncomfortable, but they are clarifying. They show where love has been present but incomplete. They show where the relationship has been trying to survive on an uneven foundation. They show what must be strengthened if the relationship is going to become more than a repetition of the same cycle. This is the final step before the relationship can become a learning system.

First, the illusion had to be challenged. Then the self-had to be seen. Then the system had to be understood. Then the pattern had to be traced over time. Now love itself has to be redefined, not as a feeling to preserve, but as a structure to develop. That redefinition changes what becomes possible.

If love is only a feeling, then its changes are frightening. If love is a system, then its changes are information. If love is only something two people have, then difficulty feels like evidence that something is being lost. If love is something two people build, then difficulty can reveal what still needs to be strengthened.

This does not mean every relationship can or should continue. Some systems are too harmful. Some are too one-sided. Some are unwilling to learn. Some contain love, but not enough safety, accountability, or mutual capacity to become healthy. Seeing what love is made of does not require romanticizing every bond.

It may clarify why a relationship cannot hold what it claims to value. But when both people are willing, this understanding becomes an invitation.

It invites them to stop defending the idea that love exists and begin developing the conditions that allow love to function. It invites them to stop treating the relationship as proof of feeling and begin treating it as a living system that needs attention, feedback, repair, and growth. It invites them to stop asking whether love is real and start asking whether love is becoming more capable over time. That is the deeper question. Not whether love once felt powerful. Not whether it still appears in moments. Not whether the relationship contains enough history to justify continuing. But whether the system can learn. Because love that cannot learn will eventually repeat what it refuses to understand. And love that can learn becomes something more than feeling, more than fantasy, more than endurance. It becomes a relationship capable of becoming wiser than it was at the beginning.

PART IV
THE LEARNING RELATIONSHIP

There is a point in the development of a relationship when the central question changes.

It is no longer only whether two people love each other. It is no longer only whether they feel connected, whether their values broadly align, or whether they want the relationship to continue. Those questions still matter, but they are no longer sufficient. By the time a relationship has moved through illusion, self-awareness, systems awareness, recurring patterns, and the attempt to become a team, a deeper question becomes unavoidable. Can this relationship learn? That question sits at the center of Part IV.

A relationship that cannot learn is forced to repeat. It may repeat conflict, distance, misunderstanding, withdrawal, defensiveness, resentment, repair attempts that never become repair, apologies that do not lead to change, and promises that restore hope without altering the system. It may contain love. It may contain commitment. It may even contain moments of genuine tenderness. But if the relationship cannot learn from what keeps happening, it remains organized around repetition. A learning relationship is different.

It is not a perfect relationship. It is not free of conflict, fear, disappointment, or strain. It does not require two people who always communicate skillfully, regulate quickly, or respond with maturity in every difficult moment. A learning relationship is one that can notice what is happening, make meaning from it, adjust behavior, repair with integrity, and become more capable over time.

This is where the principles that have been developing throughout the book begin to come together. Systems thinking allows the couple to see the pattern instead of only the event. Personal mastery allows each person to observe their own reactions inside the pattern. Mental models reveal the assumptions that shape interpretation. The movement from me to us creates the possibility of shared response. The fuller understanding of love shows that feeling alone cannot sustain what structure must support. Now the relationship has to use all of that awareness.

Chapter 9, "The Relationship as a Learning System," brings the central premise of this book fully into view. It explores why some couples keep repeating the same conflict while others become more capable because of what they have been through. It asks what happens when a relationship stops treating difficulty as interruption and begins treating it as information.

Chapter 10, "Repair, Feedback, and Adaptation," will move more directly into the practical structure of rebuilding trust, noticing drift, responding to breakdown, and using feedback without turning the relationship into a scorecard. It will examine what real repair requires once the system has been damaged.

Chapter 11, "Strategic Love," will close the book by bringing intention, direction, and design into the relationship without making love mechanical. It will ask what it means to move forward with a clearer understanding of what love is, what it requires, and how it can be built deliberately without losing its humanity.

The purpose of this final part is not to promise that every relationship can be saved. Some relationships do not have the safety, willingness, mutual accountability, or adaptive capacity required to become learning systems. Some patterns reveal not a need for more effort, but a need for clarity, boundaries, or exit. A relationship cannot learn if only one person is willing to observe, adjust, and repair. But when both people are willing, the relationship can become something more than the sum of its injuries. It can become wiser.

Not because pain is valuable by itself, and not because struggle automatically creates strength. Struggle does not make a relationship stronger unless the relationship knows how to learn from it. Without learning, struggle only repeats.

With learning, difficulty becomes a source of information, and information becomes the raw material of change. This is the difference between a relationship that survives and a relationship that evolves.

CHAPTER NINE

THE CYCLE OF LOVE

Why Some Couples Grow and Others Repeat

Every relationship has an argument that keeps coming back.

It may not look the same every time. The topic may change. One month it is about money. Another month it is about time, family, household responsibilities, intimacy, parenting, tone, attention, or the feeling that one person is carrying more than the other. On the surface, each conflict appears to be about the issue in front of it. The details shift enough to make the argument seem new. But underneath, the emotional structure is familiar.

One person feels dismissed. The other feels criticized. One feels alone. The other feels inadequate. One feels controlled. The other feels abandoned. One feels unseen. The other feels like nothing they do is enough. The words change, but the positions remain. The relationship finds its way back to the same place, as if some hidden path has been worn into the ground. This is the kind of repetition that begins to exhaust love.

Not because the couple lacks feeling. Not because there is no care, no desire, no history, no reason to continue. The exhaustion comes from the sense that nothing is changing. The same pain returns with new language. The same apology appears with new sincerity. The same temporary closeness follows the same familiar rupture. For a while, both people may believe the next conversation will be the one that finally changes things. Eventually, even hope begins to feel repetitive.

This is often the moment when people say, "We keep talking about it, but nothing changes." That sentence matters. It reveals the difference between conversation and learning (Argyris & Schön, 1978; Senge, 2006).

Many couples talk. They revisit the issue, explain their feelings, defend their intentions, apologize, promise, clarify, and try again. They may spend hours in conversations that feel emotionally intense and meaningful in the moment. There may be tears, insight, tenderness, and the temporary relief that comes when both people feel, for a little while, that they have found their way back to each other. But a conversation does not become learning simply because it is emotional. Learning requires that the system changes as a result of what was understood (Blanchard et al., 2009; Hawkins et al., 2008).

This is where many relationships get stuck. They mistake expression for transformation. They believe that because something was discussed, something has been resolved. They believe that because an apology was offered, repair has occurred. They believe that because both people felt close afterward, the pattern has shifted. But if the next stressful moment produces the same sequence, the relationship has not learned. It has only recovered.

Recovery matters. There is value in returning to connection after conflict. A relationship that cannot return at all is fragile in its own way. But recovery without learning becomes a cycle of rupture and relief. The relationship is repeatedly injured, soothed, and then placed back into the same conditions that made the injury likely. This is why nothing changes.

Not because people do not care. Often they care deeply. Not because they do not understand anything. Often they understand more than they are able to practice. Nothing changes because insight has not yet become structure. The system has not been given a new way to operate. A learning relationship begins with a different assumption. It assumes that recurring difficulty is information.

This does not mean difficulty is welcomed in some artificial or overly positive way. Pain is still pain. Conflict still hurts. Disappointment still has consequences. A learning relationship does not pretend that every rupture is useful simply because something can be learned from it. That kind of thinking can become dismissive, especially when real harm has occurred. But a learning relationship refuses to waste pain by allowing it to repeat without understanding.

When the same argument returns, the question is not only, "How do we make this stop?" It is, "What has this argument been trying to show us?" When distance appears again, the question is not only, "How do we get close again?" It is, "What keeps creating the conditions for this distance?" When one person shuts down and the other escalates, the question is not only, "Who is wrong?" It is, "What is the sequence, and how are we both helping it continue?"

These questions do not remove accountability. They deepen it. They ask each person to become responsible not only for their behavior in the moment, but for their participation in the pattern over time. This is the central difference between a repeating relationship and a learning relationship. A repeating relationship reacts to the latest event. A learning relationship studies the pattern that produced it.

In a repeating relationship, conflict confirms the existing story. If one person already believes they are not important, every missed signal becomes evidence. If the other already believes they are constantly failing, every concern becomes accusation. Each new conflict strengthens what each person already feared was true. The system becomes organized around confirmation.

In a learning relationship, conflict is treated as a signal that something in the system needs attention. The signal may be painful, but it is not automatically turned into a verdict. It is examined. The couple asks what happened, what each person made it mean, what reaction followed, what the reaction produced, and what the relationship needs in order to respond differently next time. This shift requires a different emotional posture.

It asks two people to become curious before they become certain. It asks them to pause before turning pain into evidence. It asks them to consider that the meaning their mind assigned to the moment may be only part of the truth. It asks them to look at the relationship not as a courtroom, where one person must be convicted, but as a system, where the pattern must be understood. This is difficult because the courtroom is familiar.

When people are hurt, they want the facts arranged in a way that proves the legitimacy of the hurt. They want the other person to see what they did, admit it, and repair it. These desires are not wrong. Harm should be acknowledged. Impact should be taken seriously. But if the relationship remains only at the level of proving harm, it may never reach the deeper level of understanding how the harm keeps occurring. A learning relationship must be able to do both.

It must be able to say, "This hurt," and also, "This belongs to a pattern." It must be able to say, "You are responsible for that behavior," and also, "We need to understand the system that keeps making this behavior more likely." It must be able to hold the seriousness of impact without reducing the entire relationship to blame.

That is not easy work. It requires maturity from both people, and it requires enough safety for truth to enter without being immediately punished.

In many relationships, feedback is treated as danger. One person says, "Something is not working," and the other hears, "You are failing." One person says, "I need this to change," and the other hears, "You are not enough." One person says, "I am hurt," and the other hears, "You are the problem." The feedback may be clumsy, poorly timed, or emotionally charged, but even when it is delivered with care, it activates threat. Once feedback becomes threat, learning stops.

The conversation shifts from curiosity to protection. The person receiving feedback defends, explains, withdraws, minimizes, counters, or collapses into shame. The person offering feedback feels unheard and becomes more insistent, more guarded, or less willing to bring things forward in the future. The system learns that truth is expensive. Over time, the relationship adapts by reducing feedback.

The couple may become more peaceful, but less honest. They may fight less, but not because the relationship has become healthier. They fight less because one or both people have learned that certain truths are not worth the cost of saying aloud. The system becomes quieter, but also less capable of learning. This is a dangerous kind of stability.

It looks like calm from the outside. Inside, it is often a form of contraction. The relationship has narrowed around what it can tolerate. Certain needs are no longer named. Certain disappointments are no longer raised. Certain patterns are no longer challenged. The relationship survives by excluding information that would require it to change. A learning relationship does the opposite. It builds enough capacity to let information enter.

This does not mean feedback is constant, harsh, or unfiltered. A relationship is not strengthened by turning every irritation into a discussion or every emotional shift into an analysis. Feedback must be delivered with care, timing, humility, and respect for the other person's nervous system. But a relationship that cannot receive any feedback without collapse cannot become a learning system. Feedback is how the relationship discovers itself (Edmondson, 1999; Senge, 2006).

It is how the system learns that something is drifting, that a pattern is forming, that a repair did not hold, that one person is adjusting too much, that an assumption is operating, that the shared vision is becoming unclear. Without feedback, the relationship must wait until the consequences become too large to ignore. By then, what might have been adjusted early often requires repair. The ability to receive feedback without collapse is one of the strongest indicators that a relationship can grow.

Collapse can take many forms. It can look like defensiveness, where the person immediately argues with the information. It can look like shame, where the person becomes so overwhelmed by feeling bad that the other person has to comfort them instead of addressing the issue. It can look like withdrawal, where the person leaves the emotional field. It can look like counterattack, where the feedback is met with a list of the other person's failures. It can look like intellectualization, where the person analyzes the issue at a distance without allowing its emotional truth to land. In each case, the system avoids learning.

The feedback does not become usable because the relationship becomes organized around managing the reaction to the feedback.

A learning relationship develops a different capacity. It does not require either person to enjoy feedback. Most people do not enjoy being told that their behavior has hurt someone, that a pattern is not working, or that the relationship needs something different. The point is not comfort. The point is recoverability. Can the person hear enough to remain engaged? Can they separate impact from identity? Can they say, "This is hard to hear, but I want to understand"? Can they return if they need time? Can they allow the relationship to be more important than the immediate need to protect their self-image? These moments are where learning either begins or stops.

The same is true for the person giving feedback. A learning relationship also requires that concerns be brought forward in ways the system can use. Pain does not excuse carelessness. If feedback is delivered with contempt, accusation, exaggeration, or the desire to punish, the system will respond to the threat before it can respond to the information. The concern may be valid, but the delivery may still reinforce the pattern.

This does not mean every feeling must be perfectly regulated before it can be spoken. That would make honesty impossible for many people. It means that both people must become responsible for making truth usable. One must learn to bring truth with enough care that it can be received. The other must learn to receive truth with enough steadiness that it can be considered. When both capacities are present, the relationship becomes more intelligent.

It does not need to wait for crisis. It can notice earlier. It can adjust sooner. It can use small signals before they become large injuries. It can say, "We are beginning to drift," before drift becomes distance. It can say, "This pattern is showing up again," before the pattern becomes a full rupture. It can say, "I am starting to protect myself from you," before self-protection becomes the emotional architecture of the relationship. This is what it means for a relationship to learn. Learning is not simply knowing more. It is becoming different because of what is known.

A couple may know their pattern and still repeat it. They may know that one pursues and the other withdraws. They may know that defensiveness blocks repair. They may know that conflict escalates when tone hardens. They may know that avoidance creates distance. But knowledge alone does not change a system. Knowledge must be converted into different behavior at the points where the pattern normally takes over. The first time this happens, it may feel almost too small to matter (Baer et al., 1968; Stokes & Baer, 1977).

The same conversation begins. The same tension appears. One person feels the familiar urgency to make the point more strongly. The other feels the familiar impulse to defend or disappear. The system begins to move toward the old sequence. Then someone pauses. Not dramatically. Not perfectly. Just enough.

They say, "I think we are starting to do the thing we always do." Or, "I want to respond differently here." Or, "I am hearing this as criticism, but I want to check before I react." Or, "I need a moment, but I am not leaving the conversation." Or, "I can feel myself getting defensive, and I want to understand what you are actually saying." That moment may not solve the issue. But it changes the system.

For the first time, the pattern is no longer invisible. The couple is not only inside the reaction; they are observing it while it is happening. This creates space, and space allows choice. The old sequence may still be powerful. Both people may still be activated. The conversation may still be difficult. But the relationship has done something different. It has noticed itself. Noticing is the first act of a learning system. The next act is adjustment.

Adjustment does not need to be grand. It often begins with small changes that interrupt the expected sequence. The person who usually escalates softens the opening. The person who usually withdraws names the overwhelm and commits to returning. The person who usually defends listens long enough to identify the impact. The person who usually hints at a need states it directly. The person who usually assumes asks. The person who usually apologizes quickly slows down enough to understand what repair actually requires.

These changes may feel awkward because they do not yet belong to the established system. The old pattern is smooth because it has been practiced. The new pattern is uneven because it is being built. This awkwardness should not be mistaken for failure. Often, it is the feeling of the relationship learning a movement it has not practiced before. At first, the system may resist.

If one person responds differently, the other may not immediately trust it. The partner who has experienced years of withdrawal may not relax when the withdrawer stays present once. The partner who has experienced repeated criticism may not feel safe because one concern is delivered with care. The partner who has experienced broken promises may not trust a new commitment just because it is spoken sincerely. This caution is not necessarily sabotage. It may be the relationship's memory.

A system built through repetition cannot be rebuilt through a single exception. The new behavior has to appear often enough, under enough conditions, that the relationship can begin updating what it expects. Trust changes when the system has repeated evidence that something different is becoming reliable. This is why learning requires consistency.

A relationship learns not from the best conversation a couple has ever had, but from the pattern that follows. Did the new insight change what happened next week? Did the apology alter behavior under stress? Did the difficult conversation create a new agreement that was actually practiced? Did the person who said they would return after taking space return repeatedly enough for the relationship to believe them? Learning is proven by the future.

This is where many couples become discouraged. They mistake the emotional intensity of a breakthrough for the completion of change. They have one powerful conversation and expect the relationship to feel different immediately. When the old pattern returns, they conclude that the conversation did not matter. It may have mattered. It just was not enough.

Breakthroughs can open the door, but systems change through repetition. The relationship must practice what it understood until the new pattern becomes more available than the old one. This means that the work after insight is often less dramatic than the insight itself. It is slower, quieter, and more ordinary. It happens in the next tense conversation, the next misunderstood tone, the next moment of disappointment, the next time someone needs to choose repair over pride. This is where relationships either evolve or return to what they know.

A learning relationship understands that growth is not a mood. It is not the optimism that follows a good conversation. It is the discipline of changing what happens next. That discipline must become shared.

One person can begin learning. One person can notice their own pattern, regulate their reaction, question their assumptions, and respond differently. That matters. It can change the emotional field. It can create opportunities that did not exist before. It can reveal whether the relationship has capacity for more. But one person cannot make a relationship into a learning system alone.

A learning system requires participation. If only one person observes, only one person repairs, only one person adjusts, and only one person remains accountable, the relationship does not become a learning system. It becomes an imbalanced system supported by one person's growth.

This distinction is important because many people mistake their own increased maturity for relational progress. They become calmer, clearer, more patient, more articulate, more capable of naming the pattern. The relationship may feel less chaotic because they are no longer feeding the old sequence in the same way. But if the other person remains unwilling to see, respond, repair, or change, the system itself may still be limited. Personal growth can improve the way one person moves through the relationship. Shared growth changes the relationship. A learning relationship requires both.

Not equally in every moment. There may be seasons where one person has more capacity, more awareness, or more readiness than the other. Growth is rarely perfectly synchronized. But over time, there must be mutual movement. Both people must become willing to let the relationship teach them something they did not already know. Both must allow feedback to alter behavior. Both must care not only about being understood, but about understanding the system they are creating. This shared orientation changes the experience of difficulty.

In a repeating relationship, difficulty becomes a threat to the bond. It activates fear, defensiveness, and the old question of whether the relationship is working. In a learning relationship, difficulty still hurts, but it does not automatically mean the relationship is failing. It means the system has encountered something it must understand. This is not a small difference.

It allows the couple to remain more stable while addressing instability. They do not have to interpret every conflict as proof that love is disappearing. They do not have to treat every emotional shift as a verdict. They can see difficulty as part of development, provided the difficulty is being used to increase capacity rather than being repeated without change. This is where a learning relationship becomes more resilient than a relationship built only on harmony.

Harmony can be beautiful, but harmony alone may not reveal much about the strength of the system. A couple can feel harmonious because the conditions are favorable, the differences are untested, or the difficult truths are being avoided. Resilience is revealed when harmony is disrupted and the relationship still knows how to find its way back with greater understanding. A resilient relationship is not one that never breaks rhythm. It is one that can recover rhythm without pretending nothing happened.

This requires the couple to change their relationship with rupture. Rupture is not ideal, and repeated rupture without repair is damaging. But some rupture is inevitable in any close relationship. People misunderstand each other. They react poorly. They miss cues. They disappoint. They speak from fear. They fail to see impact until after impact has occurred. The question is not whether rupture will ever happen. The question is whether rupture becomes a teacher or a recurring wound.

In a learning relationship, rupture is followed by repair that changes the system. The couple does not merely apologize and resume. They ask what broke, what made it more likely, what each person experienced, what needs to be repaired emotionally, and what must be different structurally. They do not treat repair as the end of discomfort alone. They treat it as the beginning of a new pattern. This kind of repair is demanding because it requires more than regret.

Regret looks backward and feels sorrow for what happened. Repair looks backward, understands what happened, and then looks forward to change the conditions that allowed it. Regret may say, "I feel terrible." Repair says, "I understand what I did, I understand how it affected you, and I am changing the pattern that made it possible." A learning relationship needs repair because without it, feedback has nowhere to go.

If feedback is given but nothing changes, the system learns that speaking does not matter. If pain is named but repair remains emotional rather than behavioral, the system learns that expression may create temporary closeness but not structural change. If apologies repeat without new behavior, the system learns that remorse is not reliable. Over time, this damages trust. Not only trust in the person, but trust in the relationship's capacity to learn.

There are few things more discouraging than realizing a relationship can understand the problem but not change it. The couple can name the pattern. They can explain the history. They can identify triggers. They can speak the language of growth. But when pressure returns, the system remains the same. This is the difference between insight and integration. Insight sees. Integration changes.

A learning system requires integration. The new understanding must become embedded in how the relationship functions. It must shape decisions, conversations, expectations, boundaries, and repair. It must become part of the shared operating system. This is how growth becomes a shared experience rather than an individual project.

Shared growth has a different emotional quality. It is not one person dragging the relationship toward health while the other resists. It is not two people separately working on themselves and hoping the relationship improves by implication. It is the experience of both people turning toward the same pattern and saying, in effect, "We do not want to keep creating this. What do we need to learn?" That question creates partnership.

It places the pattern in front of both people instead of between them. The couple is no longer only looking at each other as the source of pain. They are looking together at the system that has been producing pain. This does not eliminate individual responsibility, but it changes the posture. The goal is no longer to defeat the other person's version of reality. The goal is to build a shared reality accurate enough to support change. Shared growth also changes how people experience accountability.

In an immature system, accountability often feels like exposure. Someone is wrong, someone is blamed, someone must admit fault. The conversation becomes charged with fear because identity is on the line. In a learning system, accountability becomes part of development. It is still uncomfortable. It still matters. But it is not treated as humiliation. It is treated as information about where change is needed. This is what allows two people to become more honest.

They can admit, "I withdrew because I was overwhelmed, and I see how that left you alone." They can say, "I pushed harder because I was afraid, and I see how that made you feel cornered." They can say, "I apologized too quickly because I wanted the discomfort to end, not because I fully understood the impact." They can say, "I have been calling it peace, but I think I have actually been avoiding the truth." These admissions are powerful because they interrupt the performance of innocence.

Most relationships do not need perfect people. They need people who can stop pretending their patterns are harmless. They need people who can identify the difference between intention and impact, between explanation and repair, between wanting the relationship to improve and changing the behavior that keeps it from improving. This is what learning looks like at the level of the self and the system.

The individual learns, "This is what happens in me." The relationship learns, "This is what happens between us." The individual asks, "How do I enter this differently?" The relationship asks, "How do we structure this differently?" Both forms of learning matter because neither alone is enough. If the individual changes without the relationship changing, the system may remain limited. If the couple tries to change the system without individual responsibility, the new structure will not hold. A learning relationship requires both personal mastery and shared practice.

This is where the framework of the learning organization becomes deeply relevant to love. In any organization that learns well, people do not simply react to problems as they appear. They examine patterns, challenge assumptions, develop individual capacity, create shared vision, and learn together through feedback. The goal is not merely to perform better in one moment, but to become a system capable of adapting over time. A relationship needs the same capacities, translated into human terms (Senge, 2006; Argyris & Schön, 1978; Edmondson, 1999).

In organizational learning, the central question is not whether people have discussed a problem, but whether the system's underlying assumptions and patterns of action have changed. Argyris and Schön described this as the difference between correcting an error inside the existing frame and revising the frame that produced the error in the first place. A relationship faces the same choice. It can solve the visible disagreement while preserving the rules that made the disagreement inevitable, or it can let the disagreement reveal what the system itself needs to learn (Argyris & Schön, 1978; Senge, 2006).

Systems thinking allows the couple to see the whole pattern instead of isolated incidents. Personal mastery allows each person to govern themselves inside the pattern. Mental models reveal the invisible assumptions that shape meaning. Shared vision gives the relationship direction. Team learning allows both people to make use of what the relationship is showing them. When these capacities are absent, the relationship becomes reactive. When they are present, the relationship becomes adaptive.

Adaptation is one of the clearest signs that a relationship is learning. The couple does not continue applying old responses to new conditions. They notice when life has changed, when needs have changed, when the relationship has outgrown an old agreement, when a coping strategy that once worked now creates distance. They do not treat every need for adjustment as evidence of failure. They treat it as part of staying alive to the truth of the relationship. This matters because relationships do not fail only because people stop loving each other. They fail because they stop adapting to what love now requires.

The relationship that worked in one season may not work in another. The couple who communicated well before children, before illness, before career pressure, before grief, before aging parents, before financial strain, before personal growth, may need a new system under new conditions. If they assume the old pattern should still work, they may blame each other for a failure that is actually a failure of adaptation. A learning relationship expects the need for revision.

It understands that no system remains healthy by refusing to change. It asks, "What season are we in now?" "What does this stage require that the last stage did not?" "What assumptions are we still carrying from an earlier version of us?" "What do we need to stop expecting from a system that was built for conditions we no longer live in?" These questions protect the relationship from nostalgia.

Nostalgia can be tender, but it can also become a form of resistance. Couples may keep comparing the present to the beginning, or to a season when connection felt easier, and assume the task is to get back there. But a learning relationship does not aim to return to its earlier self. It aims to become more capable than its earlier self could have been. The beginning was not the goal. It was the starting point.

A relationship that learns becomes something neither person could have built at the beginning because neither person knew enough yet. They had not encountered the necessary difficulties. They had not seen the patterns. They had not discovered the meanings each brought into conflict. They had not learned where the system was fragile or where repair would be needed. This is why mature love has a different texture than early love (Senge, 2006; Daks & Rogge, 2020).

Early love often feels powerful because it is full of possibility. Mature love feels powerful because it contains evidence. Evidence that the relationship can face hard things. Evidence that both people can change. Evidence that repair is more than a performance. Evidence that feedback does not have to become collapse. Evidence that the system is not perfect, but it is alive enough to learn. This kind of love is less dependent on fantasy.

It does not need to pretend that difficulty is absent. It does not require both people to maintain idealized versions of themselves. It does not panic every time the relationship encounters strain. It has enough history with learning to know that strain can become information, and information can become growth. That confidence is not naïve. It is earned.

A couple earns it every time they interrupt an old pattern. Every time they return after needing space. Every time they listen when defensiveness would be easier. Every time they clarify instead of assume. Every time they repair with changed behavior. Every time they let the relationship tell them the truth about what it needs next. Over time, these moments accumulate. They become the new memory of the system.

Instead of expecting every hard conversation to become a fight, the relationship begins to expect that hard conversations can become understanding. Instead of expecting distance to become abandonment, the relationship begins to expect that distance can be named and repaired. Instead of expecting feedback to become shame or defense, the relationship begins to expect that feedback can lead to adjustment. The system learns new expectations because it has lived through new evidence. This is how two people become something new together.

Not by erasing their histories, and not by pretending old patterns never existed. They become something new by creating enough different experiences that the relationship develops a new way of functioning. The old patterns may still appear under stress, but they no longer have the same authority. They can be recognized sooner. They can be interrupted more often. They can be repaired more honestly. The relationship becomes less automatic. It becomes more conscious.

This does not mean it becomes heavy or constantly analytical. In fact, one of the gifts of a learning relationship is that over time, it may become lighter. Not because it avoids serious work, but because the system is no longer carrying so much unexamined material. There is less need to guess, less need to defend, less need to protect against every possible meaning. The relationship has built enough trust in its own capacity to recover that not every difficulty feels like a threat to its existence. That lightness is not the lightness of the beginning. It is the lightness that comes after structure.

It is the ease that becomes possible when two people have learned how to tell the truth without destroying the bond, how to disagree without losing the relationship, how to repair without pretending, and how to change without interpreting change as failure. This is the deeper promise of the learning relationship. Not that love will always feel easy. But that love can become more capable.

A capable relationship is not one that never suffers. It is one that knows how to use suffering wisely when suffering enters. It is not one that never repeats old patterns. It is one that recognizes repetition sooner and responds with more skill. It is not one that never injures. It is one that repairs in ways that reduce the likelihood of the same injury recurring. Capability is built through learning. And learning requires humility.

A relationship cannot learn when both people are committed to appearing already right. It cannot learn when feedback is treated as disloyalty, when apology is treated as weakness, when conflict is treated as proof of incompatibility, or when change is treated as an admission that the relationship was wrong from the beginning.

To learn, a couple must be willing to say, "We do not yet know how to do this well." That sentence is not a failure. It is an opening.

It makes room for development. It allows the couple to stop pretending that love should automatically provide skills no one has practiced. It allows both people to become students of the relationship they are trying to build.

This is where the learning relationship becomes deeply human. It does not demand that two people arrive fully formed. It asks that they remain willing to be formed by what the relationship reveals. It asks that they bring enough courage to see their patterns, enough humility to revise their assumptions, enough discipline to practice new responses, and enough care to keep the shared system from becoming a place where old wounds are simply reenacted. Not every relationship can do this.

Some are too unsafe. Some are too one-sided. Some are organized around denial, control, contempt, or avoidance so deeply that learning cannot take root. Some people want the benefits of being loved without the responsibility of becoming more conscious inside love. Some want the relationship to improve without allowing their own behavior to be altered by what the relationship has shown them. A learning relationship cannot be built from unwillingness.

It requires consent from both people, not only to remain together, but to keep becoming more honest about what togetherness requires.

When that willingness is present, the relationship begins to change in ways that are both practical and profound. The same conflict does not have to mean the same thing. The same wound does not have to reopen in the same way. The same fear does not have to govern the next decision. The same silence does not have to become the same distance. The same apology does not have to lead to the same disappointment. The relationship gains a future that is not simply a repetition of its past. That future is built through learning.

It is built when two people understand that love is not weakened by being examined. It is strengthened when examination leads to greater care. It is built when the relationship can receive feedback without turning it into a war. It is built when each person can see themselves inside the system without collapsing into shame or escaping into blame. It is built when repair becomes behavioral, not merely emotional. It is built when the couple stops asking, "Why does this keep happening to us?" and begins asking, "What do we need to learn so this does not keep happening through us?" That question changes everything.

It shifts the relationship from fate to participation. From reaction to awareness. From repetition to adaptation. From emotional survival to relational growth.

The argument that keeps coming back is no longer only a source of exhaustion. It becomes a signal. The pattern that once felt inevitable becomes visible. The injury that once led only to distance becomes a place where repair can become more exact. The relationship that once repeated itself begins, slowly, to become more intelligent. This is not a sentimental view of love. It is a demanding one.

It asks more than feeling. It asks more than staying. It asks more than good intentions. It asks two people to become capable of learning from the relationship they are creating together. But that demand is also what gives love its possibility.

Because if a relationship can learn, then it is not trapped inside the limits of its beginning. It is not confined to the patterns each person brought into it unconsciously. It is not doomed to repeat every old interpretation, every inherited fear, every defensive habit, every failed repair. It can become something more developed than what either person knew how to build at first. A learning relationship does not promise that love will never hurt. It promises that hurt does not have to be wasted. It does not promise that conflict will disappear. It promises that conflict can become information. It does not promise that both people will always know what to do. It promises that when they do not know, they can learn. That is the difference between couples who grow and couples who repeat.

The couples who repeat are not always less loving. They are often less able to learn from the places where love is asking for development. The couples who grow are not free from difficulty. They are willing to let difficulty change them in ways that make the relationship more truthful, more capable, and more alive. This is where love becomes more than something two people feel. It becomes a system that can observe itself, correct itself, and evolve. It becomes a relationship capable of becoming wiser than it was at the beginning.

CHAPTER TEN

REPAIR, FEEDBACK, AND ADAPTATION

How the System Begins to Hold Again

There is a stage in many relationships when both people know something has changed, but neither can yet name exactly what has broken.

The relationship continues. Conversations still happen. Routines remain in place. Affection may still appear in familiar ways. There may be ordinary kindness, shared responsibilities, moments of humor, even stretches of calm that make the problem seem less urgent than it is. From the outside, nothing may look especially damaged. But inside the relationship, the atmosphere has shifted. Something feels less safe. Less open. Less certain.

It may not feel like a crisis. At least not at first. It may feel like hesitation. A slight delay before saying what would once have been said easily. A carefulness that was not there before. A decision to leave something alone because bringing it up feels too costly. A moment of disappointment that is swallowed rather than shared. A quiet adjustment in what one person expects from the other. This is how drift begins.

Drift is not always dramatic. It often begins in the small places where the relationship stops telling the truth about itself. One person decides not to mention something because the timing is not right. Another avoids a conversation because they are tired. Someone accepts an apology that did not fully repair the injury because they do not want to keep fighting. Someone notices a pattern returning but convinces themselves it is not worth naming again. Each moment seems manageable in isolation. Together, they begin to change the system.

The danger of drift is that it rarely announces itself as danger. It does not always feel like rupture. It feels like adaptation. A person becomes less expressive, but calls it maturity. Another becomes less expectant, but calls it acceptance. Someone stops asking for reassurance, but not because trust has grown. They stop because asking has begun to feel humiliating. Someone stops bringing up the recurring issue, but not because it has been resolved. They stop because the relationship has taught them that naming it will not lead to change. The relationship becomes quieter. But quieter is not always healthier. Sometimes quiet means the system is holding. Sometimes quiet means the system has stopped receiving feedback. A relationship cannot repair what it is no longer allowed to know.

This is why feedback matters. Not feedback as criticism, surveillance, or constant evaluation, but feedback as the relationship's way of staying in contact with itself. Feedback is the information that tells the system whether it is strengthening or weakening, whether trust is growing or eroding, whether closeness is real or only performed, whether peace is the result of repair or the result of avoidance.

Without feedback, a relationship is forced to rely on assumption. One person assumes the issue has passed because it has not been mentioned. The other assumes the silence should be obvious evidence that something remains unresolved. One assumes the apology repaired the harm. The other accepted the apology because they had no energy left to keep explaining the harm. One assumes the relationship is stable because conflict has decreased. The other experiences the decrease in conflict as emotional withdrawal. Both people may be living in different versions of the same relationship. Feedback is how those versions are brought into the room (Edmondson, 1999; Senge, 2006).

This does not mean every discomfort needs to become a conversation. A relationship that treats every passing feeling as a crisis becomes exhausting. Not every irritation is a pattern. Not every shift in mood carries deep meaning. Not every disappointment requires immediate processing. Part of relational maturity is knowing the difference between a temporary emotional state and information the relationship needs in order to remain healthy.

But the opposite mistake is more common and more damaging over time. People minimize what deserves attention. They tell themselves the issue is too small, too familiar, too inconvenient, too likely to create conflict. They wait for the right time, and the right time never arrives. They choose peace in the moment and pay for it in distance later. The relationship does not break only from what people say badly. It also breaks from what they stop saying entirely.

The slow drift often begins there. Not with betrayal, not with a dramatic argument, not with a single wound from which the relationship cannot recover. It begins with the gradual loss of usable truth. The system continues operating, but with less information. Needs are muted. Resentments become private. Questions are held back. Feedback disappears from the relationship and reappears as mood, distance, irritability, fantasy, numbness, or quiet grief. By the time the problem becomes visible, it may feel sudden. It rarely is.

What looks like sudden collapse is often accumulated unresponsiveness. The relationship was signaling distress long before either person was willing or able to respond. The signals were there in the recurring argument, the unresolved apology, the careful silence, the lack of follow-through, the tension around certain topics, the change in how people entered the room with each other. A system usually speaks before it breaks. The question is whether anyone is listening.

Listening to the system requires paying attention to more than major conflict. It requires noticing the smaller changes that reveal how the relationship is functioning. Do difficult conversations lead to greater clarity, or do they end because someone runs out of energy? Do apologies change behavior, or only soften the moment? Does taking space lead to return, or does it become a way to avoid repair? Does peace feel connected, or does it feel like both people are managing themselves carefully to avoid another rupture?

These questions are not meant to turn love into measurement in the cold sense. They are meant to protect love from the damage of inattention. Every serious system requires some form of feedback. Businesses track performance because intention does not guarantee effectiveness. Teams review outcomes because effort does not guarantee alignment. Human bodies send signals long before breakdown becomes undeniable. Relationships are no different. They have signals, too. The challenge is that relational signals are often emotional, subtle, and easy to misread.

A partner's irritability may be dismissed as stress. It may be stress. It may also be the early sign of unmet need. A decrease in affection may be explained by fatigue. It may be fatigue. It may also be the visible effect of unresolved hurt. Silence may be interpreted as peace. It may be peace. It may also be resignation. The same behavior can mean different things in different systems, which is why feedback must be spoken rather than guessed. A learning relationship does not rely only on interpretation. It asks.

Not in a suspicious way. Not in a way that interrogates every mood. It asks because the relationship matters enough not to be left entirely to assumption. It asks because two people who are trying to build something durable cannot afford to let distance become the first clear evidence that something needed attention. The question may be simple. Are we okay in the way we seem, okay?

That question can reveal more than a long argument. It creates room for the difference between external calm and internal repair. It allows one person to say, "We are not fighting, but I do not feel close." It allows another to say, "I thought we moved past this, but I am still carrying it." It allows the relationship to detect drift before drift becomes a new normal.

This kind of feedback can be uncomfortable because it interrupts the illusion of stability. Many people prefer not to know what is quietly weakening until they have no choice. But avoidance does not preserve the relationship. It preserves the conditions under which the relationship continues to weaken without intervention. Feedback is not the enemy of stability. It is one of the ways stability is maintained.

Still, feedback alone does not repair. Feedback only reveals what the system must address. Repair begins when the information is taken seriously enough to change the pattern.

This distinction is critical because many relationships confuse acknowledgment with repair. One person finally names the hurt. The other listens, perhaps even with sincerity. There is an emotional exchange. Someone apologizes. There may be tears, reassurance, tenderness, and the relief of finally having said what had been sitting beneath the surface. The relationship feels lighter for a while. But the pattern remains unchanged. Then the same injury returns (Gottman & Levenson, 1992; Baucom et al., 2011).

The next time, the hurt is not only about the original behavior. It is about the fact that the behavior continued after being named. This second injury often cuts deeper than the first because it carries a different meaning. The first time may have felt like misunderstanding. The second time begins to feel like disregard. Repeated harm after feedback changes the emotional reality of the relationship. It teaches the system that being understood is not the same as being responded to. This is why saying sorry is never enough by itself.

An apology matters when it acknowledges impact, accepts responsibility, and opens the door to repair. But an apology that does not lead to changed behavior becomes part of the pattern it claims to address. It may reduce discomfort in the moment. It may restore temporary closeness. It may reassure both people that the relationship still has tenderness in it. But if the behavior continues, the apology begins to lose its meaning. Eventually, the injured person stops hearing regret. They hear prediction.

They know the apology will come. They know the emotion will soften. They know the relationship may feel better for a few days. They also know, somewhere in the body, that the pattern has not changed enough to trust the repair. This is how apology becomes theater, even when the feeling behind it is sincere.

The person apologizing may genuinely feel remorse. They may genuinely wish they had not caused pain. But remorse is not the same as repair. Remorse is an emotional response to what happened. Repair is a behavioral response to what must now change.

The difference matters because trust is not rebuilt through emotional intensity. It is rebuilt through repeated evidence.

Trust is a system memory. It remembers what has happened often enough to become expected. If honesty has repeatedly led to defensiveness, the system expects defensiveness. If vulnerability has repeatedly led to dismissal, the system expects dismissal. If promises have repeatedly been followed by inconsistency, the system expects inconsistency. Trust does not update because someone insists the pattern is over. It updates when the relationship experiences a different pattern long enough to believe it (Skinner, 1953; Gottman & Levenson, 1992).

Behaviorally, this is why repair has to be more than remorse. The relationship updates through repeated contact with different consequences. If honesty used to produce defensiveness, honesty must now repeatedly encounter listening. If taking space used to become disappearance, taking space must now repeatedly include return. If apology used to end the discomfort without changing behavior, apology must now become the beginning of a different pattern. Trust is rebuilt when the system has enough new evidence to expect something else (Stokes & Baer, 1977; Baucom et al., 2011).

This is why the person who has caused harm often wants the relationship to move faster than it can. They may feel the force of their own regret and believe that regret should count as proof of change. They may want their partner to recognize the sincerity of the apology, to soften, to trust, to stop bringing up what happened. From the inside, the desire makes sense. They are no longer in the same emotional place. They have understood something. They want relief from the identity of having caused pain. But the relationship does not heal at the speed of the offender's remorse. It heals at the speed of rebuilt trust. That speed is often slower.

The person who was hurt is not simply responding to the latest apology. They are responding to the history that made the apology necessary. Their caution may not be punishment. It may be the system protecting itself from premature trust. To demand immediate restoration is to misunderstand what repair requires. Repair asks the person who caused harm to tolerate the lag between effort and trust.

This is one of the hardest parts of rebuilding. A person may begin doing the work and still encounter doubt. They may respond differently and still not be believed immediately. They may apologize sincerely and still hear pain. They may change and still face the emotional residue of who they have been in the relationship. That residue is not erased by explanation. It is slowly displaced by evidence.

Repair becomes real when effort becomes visible under the conditions where the old pattern used to appear. The defensive person listens when feedback is uncomfortable. The avoidant person returns when space has been taken. The inconsistent person follows through when no one is monitoring. The critical person speaks with care when frustration rises. The person who used apology as escape stays long enough to understand impact. Repair is not proven in the moment of regret. It is proven at the next point of temptation (Stokes & Baer, 1977; Wolf, 1978).

Every pattern has a point of temptation. The moment when the old response would be easier. The moment when withdrawal would reduce discomfort, when defensiveness would protect identity, when criticism would discharge anger, when silence would avoid conflict, when reassurance would be demanded rather than requested, when accountability would be softened by explanation. Repair requires a different response at that point. Not once. Repeatedly. The system must encounter the new response where the old one used to live.

This is why repair is both personal and structural. The person must change their behavior, but the relationship must also change the conditions that allowed the pattern to continue. If one person has repeatedly withdrawn, repair may require not only a promise to stop withdrawing but a clear structure for taking space and returning. If conflict has repeatedly escalated, repair may require new agreements about timing, tone, and how either person can pause the conversation without abandoning it. If feedback has repeatedly led to defensiveness, repair may require a new practice of listening for impact before explaining intent. A relationship cannot repair by hoping both people will simply do better. It needs a new structure for the moments where doing better has historically failed (Jacobson et al., 2000; Christensen et al., 2010).

This is where many couples underestimate the work. They believe that because they understand the problem, structure should no longer be necessary. But understanding is often weakest precisely when the nervous system is most activated. In the moment of stress, people rarely rise to their highest insight. They fall back on the patterns that are most practiced. Structure exists to protect the relationship when insight is not enough. This does not make love mechanical. It makes love supported.

A couple who agrees that taking space must include a clear time of return is not making the relationship cold. They are protecting against abandonment and escalation. A couple who agrees that feedback must begin with specific behavior rather than global character judgments is not making love clinical. They are protecting against shame and defensiveness. A couple who agrees to revisit unresolved issues when both are regulated is not avoiding spontaneity. They are giving truth a better chance of being heard. Structure is not the opposite of care. It is care made repeatable.

The relationship begins to hold again when care becomes reliable under pressure. Anyone can be tender when the conditions are easy. Repair asks whether tenderness can survive the moments when the relationship is strained. Anyone can promise change when the possibility of loss is close. Repair asks whether change continues when the crisis has passed. Anyone can feel remorse after causing pain. Repair asks whether remorse becomes a different pattern. This is why feedback must continue after the apology.

Many couples treat apology as the end of the conversation. In reality, apology is often the beginning of the repair process. The system still needs to know whether the new behavior is occurring, whether the injured person feels the difference, whether the agreement is holding, whether something remains unaddressed, and whether the relationship is adapting or merely calming down. Without follow-up, the relationship relies again on assumption.

One person assumes the repair is working because they are trying. The other may still feel unsafe but hesitate to say so because they do not want to discourage the effort or reopen the wound. The person trying may feel unappreciated. The person hurting may feel alone. The system drifts back into silence, only now with the added pressure of pretending that repair is underway. A learning relationship keeps repair visible.

It does not obsess over the wound, but it does not abandon it prematurely. It allows both people to ask, "Is this helping?" "What still feels unresolved?" "What has changed?" "Where are we still repeating?" "What do we need to adjust?" These questions are not accusations. They are feedback loops for repair. Repair without feedback becomes guesswork. Feedback without repair becomes exhaustion. The two must work together (Edmondson, 1999; Baucom et al., 2011).

Adaptation is what happens when feedback and repair begin to change the system. The relationship stops applying the same old responses to the same recurring problems. It revises. It adjusts. It recognizes that what was once tolerable may no longer be healthy, that what once worked may no longer fit, that what one person thought they were offering may not be what the relationship actually needs.

Adaptation is often less dramatic than people expect. It may look like changing when hard conversations happen because late-night conflict repeatedly becomes unproductive. It may look like learning that one person needs time to process, but that time must be bounded so it does not become disappearance. It may look like changing how affection is expressed because one person has been relying on intention while the other needs visible follow-through. It may look like renegotiating roles, expectations, routines, or emotional responsibilities as the relationship enters a new season. Adaptation is the relationship's refusal to remain loyal to a structure that no longer serves it.

Without adaptation, couples often keep trying harder at the wrong thing. They communicate more but not differently. They apologize often but do not repair. They stay committed to routines that preserve efficiency while draining intimacy. They keep using strategies that once reduced conflict but now prevent honesty. They call this effort because effort is present. But effort that does not adapt becomes another form of repetition. A relationship does not need more of what already is not working. It needs a different way of working.

This is where measuring what matters becomes important, but it must be done carefully. Love cannot be reduced to a scorecard. A relationship is not a dashboard of metrics, and partners are not performance units. The goal is not to quantify intimacy until it becomes sterile or to track every interaction as though the relationship were a project under audit. But there is a difference between reducing love to measurement and refusing to notice what love is showing. Some things should be paid attention to.

How often do difficult conversations end with greater understanding rather than exhaustion? How often do apologies lead to changed behavior? How often does one person feel they have to mute themselves to keep the peace? How quickly does the relationship recover after tension? How safe does each person feel bringing forward discomfort? How often does affection appear without being used to avoid accountability? These are not numbers as much as signals. They reveal the condition of the system.

A couple does not need a formal tracking method to benefit from this awareness. They need enough honesty to observe whether the relationship is becoming more capable or merely more familiar. They need to notice whether the same issue is returning with the same emotional injury. They need to distinguish between calm and avoidance, between closeness and relief, between apology and repair. The weight of small things becomes visible over time.

A single missed bid for connection may not matter much. A pattern of missed bids changes the climate. A single interrupted conversation may be understandable. A pattern of unresolved conversations changes trust. A single defensive response may be human. A pattern of defensiveness changes what can be safely said. Small things become large not because each one is catastrophic, but because repetition gives them structure. Relationships are built and damaged in increments.

People often wait for the large event because large events are easier to justify as important. But by the time the large event occurs, the system may have been weakened by years of smaller signals that went unanswered. The dramatic rupture becomes the moment everyone can point to, but the relationship may have been asking for attention long before. Paying attention before it breaks is one of the most mature acts of love.

It requires caring about the early signal. It requires taking seriously the sentence, "Something feels off," before that feeling becomes a hardened conclusion. It requires responding to feedback before feedback becomes accusation. It requires making changes before the other person has to threaten distance in order to be believed. A relationship that only changes under threat teaches both people that pain must become severe before it matters. That is a dangerous lesson.

It creates a system where one person has to escalate, withdraw, or break down before the other recognizes the seriousness of what has been said. Over time, this erodes trust not only in the partner but in the relationship's responsiveness. The injured person learns that calm honesty is not enough. The other person learns to respond only when consequences become imminent. Both are trained by the system, and the system becomes increasingly reactive. A learning relationship tries to respond earlier.

It treats early feedback as care, not inconvenience. It understands that a concern raised before collapse is an attempt to protect the relationship from greater damage. It does not punish the person who notices drift. It does not make them prove the problem is severe enough to deserve attention. It recognizes that by the time someone says, "I do not know how much longer I can do this," many earlier opportunities for repair may already have been missed.

This is not an argument for panic. Not every concern is urgent. Not every discomfort is evidence of danger. But repeated concerns deserve repeated attention, especially when they point to the same underlying pattern. Patterns are the relationship's data.

When the same issue returns, the relationship is offering information. When one person keeps naming the same hurt, the system is offering information. When an apology keeps addressing the same behavior, the system is offering information. When peace depends on one person saying less, the system is offering information. The question is whether the information will be used.

Using it well requires humility from both people. The person offering feedback must be willing to bring it forward with as much clarity and care as possible. The person receiving feedback must be willing to hear it without immediately reducing it to accusation. Both must be willing to ask what the feedback reveals about the system, not merely what it proves about one person's failure.

This is difficult because feedback touches identity. To hear that the relationship feels unsafe, distant, or painful can activate shame, defensiveness, fear, or anger. A person may want to argue with the feedback because accepting it feels like accepting a verdict against themselves. But feedback is not always a verdict. Often, it is an invitation to see the system before the system hardens further.

A person with relational maturity can say, "I do not fully see it yet, but I want to understand." That sentence can change the trajectory of a relationship.

It does not require immediate agreement. It does not require one person to abandon their own experience. It simply keeps the system open long enough for understanding to become possible. In contrast, the sentence "That is not what I meant" often closes the system too quickly. Intention matters, but it is not the whole story. Repair requires enough humility to understand impact before defending intention. Impact is where the relationship lives.

Intention lives inside the person. Impact lives between people. A relationship is shaped by the between. This is why someone can intend love and create distance, intend honesty and create fear, intend peace and create silence, intend protection and create exclusion. The gap between intention and impact is one of the most important spaces for repair.

A learning relationship does not ignore intention. It uses intention as information. But it does not allow intention to erase impact. Instead, it asks, "How did what I meant become what you experienced?" That question is far more useful than arguing over whether the hurt should have happened. It creates a bridge between the internal world of one person and the lived experience of the other. Repair often begins on that bridge.

It begins when one person can say, "I see that what I intended is not what landed." It deepens when they can say, "I want to understand what it was like for you." It becomes real when they can say, "Here is what I will do differently so the pattern does not keep repeating." The last sentence matters most. Without it, repair remains incomplete.

A relationship cannot hold on empathy alone. Empathy helps the injured person feel seen. It softens the emotional field. It creates connection. But empathy that does not lead to changed behavior becomes painful in its own way. The person feels understood but still unsafe. They hear care but still live with the same pattern. Over time, even empathy can begin to feel like another temporary state that never becomes structure. The system starts to hold again when empathy becomes reliable action.

This is often slow work. It happens one piece at a time. A conversation that used to end in withdrawal now includes a return. A concern that used to trigger defensiveness now receives a pause and a question. A pattern that used to be noticed only after damage now gets named earlier. A promise that used to remain general becomes specific enough to be practiced. The relationship begins collecting different evidence.

At first, the evidence may feel fragile. Both people may be cautious. The old pattern may still appear. There may be moments of regression, misattunement, and discouragement. This does not mean repair has failed. It means the system is learning under conditions where the old pattern is still available. Repair does not require flawless progress. It requires honest return.

When the old pattern appears again, a learning relationship does not use that as proof that nothing has changed. It asks what happened, where the system slipped, and how repair can happen sooner next time. It distinguishes between relapse into an old pattern and refusal to change the pattern. Those are not the same. A person who falls into an old response and then takes responsibility is not in the same position as a person who repeats the old response and denies its significance. The difference is learning.

This distinction protects the relationship from perfectionism. If every mistake is treated as evidence that repair is impossible, the system becomes brittle. People become afraid to try because any imperfect attempt may be judged as failure. But if repeated mistakes are excused without consequence, the system becomes unsafe. The relationship needs a middle ground: enough grace for growth, enough accountability for trust. Grace without accountability weakens repair. Accountability without grace makes repair feel dangerous. A relationship begins to hold when both are present.

This balance is especially important when trust has been damaged. The person rebuilding trust must understand that consistency is not optional. The person receiving repair must be allowed to have a slower emotional process than the person offering repair might prefer. At the same time, if the relationship is going to continue, there must eventually be room for new evidence to matter. If no amount of changed behavior can ever update the system, then the relationship may remain organized around the wound indefinitely. Repair requires both memory and openness.

Memory protects the relationship from pretending the injury did not happen. Openness allows the relationship to register when something genuinely different is happening. Without memory, repair becomes denial. Without openness, repair becomes impossible.

This is why some relationships cannot be repaired. Not because love is absent, but because the necessary conditions are not present. If harm continues, if accountability is refused, if one person is required to absorb the entire burden of repair, if feedback is punished, if boundaries are violated, if the relationship is unsafe, then repair language can become a way of delaying the truth. Some systems do not need more patience. They need protection.

A mature framework must make room for that reality. Seeing relationships as systems does not mean every system should be preserved. Some patterns are damaging enough that the healthiest adaptation is distance. Some relationships reveal that one person is willing to learn and the other is not. Some apologies are used to reset access without changing behavior. Some feedback has been given so many times without response that the issue is no longer awareness, but unwillingness. Repair requires participation. Without participation, one person's effort becomes maintenance of a system that continues to injure them.

This is why repair must be evaluated not by words alone but by the direction of the system. Is the relationship becoming more honest, more safe, more accountable, more capable? Are both people participating in the work? Does feedback lead to change? Does change endure beyond the crisis? Does the relationship become stronger because of what it has learned, or does it merely become quiet until the next rupture? These questions clarify what hope can sometimes obscure.

Hope is important, but hope should not be asked to replace evidence. A person may hope the relationship will change because they love the other person, because there is history, because the good moments are real, because the thought of ending feels unbearable. Hope can sustain people through difficult work. But hope without evidence becomes a way of remaining loyal to potential while living inside the same pattern. A repairing relationship needs hope. It also needs data.

Not cold data. Relational data. The lived evidence of what is actually changing. The nervous system notices this evidence long before the mind fully trusts it. It notices whether the tone is different. Whether return happens. Whether promises are kept. Whether truth is safer. Whether the same issue requires less force to be taken seriously. Whether the relationship can hold feedback without collapsing. Over time, this evidence begins to change the emotional climate.

The injured person may not have to brace as quickly. The person who used to defend may feel less threatened by feedback because they have practiced receiving it. The couple may move through conflict with less fear because the system has experienced repair that actually repaired. Trust begins to return, not as a decision forced by willpower, but as an expectation supported by repeated experience. The system starts to hold again.

This holding is not the same as going back. That distinction matters. Many couples imagine repair as a return to the relationship before the injury, before the drift, before the pattern became visible. But real repair rarely returns a relationship to what it was. If repair is successful, the relationship becomes different. More conscious. More honest. Less dependent on illusion. Less able to pretend that silence is safety or that affection is repair. There may be grief in that.

The old innocence may not come back. The relationship may no longer have the same untested ease. But something more durable can take its place: earned trust, tested repair, clearer structure, and the knowledge that the system can survive truth. This is the kind of holding that matters. Not the holding of denial. The holding of capacity.

A relationship that holds does not mean nothing hurts. It means hurt can be brought into a system that knows how to respond. It does not mean conflict disappears. It means conflict does not automatically become rupture. It does not mean feedback feels pleasant. It means feedback can be used. It does not mean trust is never strained. It means trust can be repaired through behavior that becomes reliable over time. This is how repair, feedback, and adaptation work together. Feedback tells the relationship what is happening. Repair responds to what has been damaged. Adaptation changes the system so the same damage is less likely to repeat.

If feedback is missing, the relationship cannot see itself. If repair is missing, the relationship cannot heal what feedback reveals. If adaptation is missing, repair becomes temporary because the old conditions remain intact. All three are necessary. Together, they move the relationship from repetition toward resilience.

This is the work that follows the learning relationship. Once two people can see the pattern, they must decide what they will do with the information. Seeing alone does not heal. Naming alone does not rebuild. Understanding alone does not make the system hold. The relationship must be changed by what it has learned.

That change is built through attention to drift, through feedback that enters before collapse, through repair that becomes behavior, through adaptation that makes old patterns less inevitable. None of this makes love less human. It makes love more responsible.

It honors the fact that people hurt each other, often unintentionally, and that intention does not erase the need for repair. It honors the fact that trust is delicate, not because it is weak, but because it is built from repeated experience. It honors the fact that relationships need structure, not because feeling is unimportant, but because feeling alone cannot carry the full weight of relational life. Love that refuses feedback becomes fragile. Love that avoids repair becomes performative. Love that cannot adapt becomes trapped in its own history.

But love that can receive feedback, repair honestly, and adapt over time becomes stronger than the version of love that depends on everything going well. It becomes capable of surviving reality.

That is where the system begins to hold again. Not because it is untouched, not because it has returned to the beginning, and not because both people have finally become perfect. It holds because it has learned how to respond to strain without denying it, how to repair damage without minimizing it, and how to change the conditions that made the damage likely. The relationship becomes less dependent on hope alone. It begins to trust its own capacity.

And once a relationship has learned how to hold, the final question becomes how it will move forward. Not by accident. Not by drift. Not by simply hoping the old patterns do not return. But with intention. With direction. With a clearer understanding of what love is asking to become.

CHAPTER ELEVEN

WHAT LOVE IS ACTUALLY MADE OF

The Way You Move Forward

By the time love becomes visible as a system, innocence is no longer available in the same way.

This does not mean love becomes less beautiful. It does not mean tenderness disappears, mystery is reduced, or the relationship becomes a project stripped of feeling. It means the old passivity can no longer be trusted. Once you understand that relationships are shaped by patterns, feedback, assumptions, behavior, repair, and adaptation, you can no longer honestly treat love as something that simply happens and then hope it continues to happen well. Something changes when the system becomes visible.

You begin to see how much of love has been left to accident. Not because people do not care, but because they have been taught to believe that care should be enough. They enter relationships with longing, attraction, sincerity, and good intentions. They want connection. They want trust. They want companionship and stability and a future that feels shared. But they often do not ask how that future will be built. They do not ask what patterns will govern it, what assumptions will shape it, what happens when stress enters, what repair will require, or what kind of structure love will need when feeling alone is no longer enough. They wing it.

Most relationships are not intentionally designed. They are gradually assembled out of whatever each person brings, whatever the early connection rewards, whatever conflict teaches them to avoid, whatever habits reduce discomfort, and whatever patterns are repeated often enough to become normal. Over time, the relationship becomes something, but not always something either person consciously chose. That is one of the quiet tragedies of love. People often wake up inside a relationship they never meant to build.

They intended trust, but built caution. They intended closeness, but built management. They intended honesty, but built a system where truth felt too expensive. They intended partnership, but built parallel lives inside a shared commitment. They intended peace, but built silence. They intended loyalty, but built endurance without growth.

None of this usually happens all at once. It happens through small, repeated acts of non-design. A difficult conversation is postponed. A need is hinted at rather than named. A pattern is noticed but not addressed. An apology is accepted before repair has occurred. A value is assumed to be shared but never defined. A recurring injury is treated as a personality difference rather than a system problem. Each moment seems minor enough to survive. Together, they become architecture. The relationship is always being designed. The only question is whether it is being designed consciously. Strategic love begins with that recognition.

The word strategic can sound strange when placed beside love. It may suggest calculation, manipulation, efficiency, or emotional distance. It may seem too cold for something as human as partnership. But strategy, properly understood, is not the enemy of love. Strategy is direction. It is the discipline of aligning what you do with what you say matters. It is the refusal to let habit, fear, urgency, and inherited patterns make decisions on behalf of the relationship. Strategic love is not love without feeling. It is love with direction.

ACT's language of values clarifies this point. Values are not goals that can be checked off once and forgotten; they are chosen directions that organize behavior over time. Strategic love asks partners to identify the kind of relationship they are trying to build and then practice behaviors consistent with that direction, especially when old habits offer faster relief. This is why committed action matters. A relationship becomes values-driven only when its repeated behaviors begin to reflect what it claims to value (Hayes et al., 2012; Daks & Rogge, 2020).

It is the difference between hoping the relationship will hold and building the conditions that allow it to hold. It is the difference between reacting to drift after it has created distance and noticing early enough to respond. It is the difference between saying, "We love each other, so we will figure it out," and asking, "What does our love require in order to remain honest, safe, adaptive, and alive?" That question changes everything.

It moves love out of fantasy without removing its humanity. It allows the relationship to become intentional without becoming mechanical. It treats partnership not as a fixed state but as a living system that needs attention, feedback, repair, and direction.

The relationship you want and the relationship you build are not always the same. This is one of the central truths of the entire book, and it becomes unavoidable here. What you want may be sincere. You may want emotional safety, trust, communication, intimacy, steadiness, and mutual growth. But wanting those things does not automatically create them. The relationship is built through repeated behavior, not through preferred identity. You may want honesty, but if difficult truth is punished, the system will learn caution. You may want closeness, but if vulnerability is met with correction, the system will learn protection. You may want peace, but if peace depends on avoidance, the system will learn silence.

You may want partnership, but if stress is handled privately until it spills into resentment, the system will learn separation. You may want repair, but if apology does not become changed behavior, the system will learn distrust.

A strategic relationship does not measure itself only by what it values. It measures itself by whether its patterns support those values. That is the difference between aspiration and design. Aspiration says what matters. Design asks whether the relationship is organized in a way that makes what matters more likely.

This is where many couples become uncomfortable, because the gap between values and structure can be painful to see. It is easier to say, "We value communication," than to notice that one person becomes defensive every time feedback is offered and the other has stopped bringing concerns forward. It is easier to say, "We value trust," than to notice that the relationship still operates around monitoring, testing, secrecy, or inconsistency. It is easier to say, "We are committed," than to ask whether the commitment is helping love grow or merely helping the relationship continue. Strategic love asks these questions anyway. Not to accuse. To align.

Alignment is one of the most important functions of mature love. It does not mean two people become identical. It does not mean they want the same thing in every moment, process emotions the same way, or carry the same needs. Alignment means the relationship has a shared direction clear enough to organize difference. It means both people understand what they are trying to build and are willing to examine whether their behavior supports that shared aim.

Without alignment, effort becomes scattered. One person may be working toward emotional closeness while the other is working toward stability through reduced conflict. One may be seeking growth while the other is seeking relief from pressure. One may interpret honesty as direct expression, while the other interprets love as restraint. Both may be trying, but they are not trying toward the same thing. This is why shared vision matters.

A shared vision is not a romantic fantasy about the future. It is not a vague dream of happiness, longevity, or togetherness. It is a practical understanding of the kind of relationship two people are choosing to build. It answers questions that many couples leave to assumption. What kind of emotional climate do we want to live in? How do we want truth to function here? What does repair require from us? How will we handle difference without turning it into threat? What do we want the relationship to make possible in each of our lives? These questions may sound simple, but they are rarely answered clearly (Senge, 2006; Ryan & Deci, 2000).

Many couples have plans. They may plan finances, homes, careers, children, schedules, vacations, or long-term goals. But a plan is not the same as a shared vision. A plan organizes tasks. A vision organizes meaning. A couple can be highly coordinated around logistics and still unclear about the kind of relationship those logistics are meant to support. They can build a life and still neglect the system that holds it.

Strategic love refuses to confuse activity with direction. It asks not only what the couple is doing, but what the couple is becoming through what they repeatedly do. It asks whether the relationship is becoming more honest, more capable, more connected, more adaptive, more respectful of both individuality and interdependence. It asks whether time is deepening the system or merely extending it.

This kind of love requires conversations that many people avoid because they feel unromantic, inconvenient, or risky. Yet these are often the conversations that protect romance from becoming a fragile surface over an unclear structure.

The conversations that matter are not only about problems. They are about definitions. What does commitment mean here? What does loyalty require? What does it not require? What does space mean? What does emotional safety mean? What does respect look like during disagreement? What does repair look like after harm? What kind of honesty do we owe each other, and how do we make that honesty usable rather than destructive?

These conversations do not remove uncertainty. They reduce unnecessary ambiguity. They give the relationship language. They help two people discover where they have been using the same words while living inside different meanings. A relationship becomes stronger when fewer things have to be guessed.

Guessing is expensive. It consumes emotional energy. It invites projection. It allows old mental models to fill in the blanks. In the absence of clarity, the mind will create meaning from whatever material is available: history, fear, prior injury, family conditioning, unmet longing, and the latest emotional state. This does not make people irrational. It makes them human. But a relationship built on too much guessing becomes vulnerable to interpretations that neither person intended but both begin to live under. Strategic love does not assume clarity will happen naturally. It builds clarity deliberately.

This does not mean every aspect of the relationship must be talked to death. There is a kind of over-processing that can make love feel heavy and self-conscious. A relationship needs room for ease, humor, spontaneity, silence, play, and the ordinary grace of not examining every moment. But ease is more sustainable when the important things have enough structure. Spontaneity is safer when the system is trustworthy. Silence is more peaceful when it does not have to carry everything unsaid. Structure does not eliminate freedom. It protects the conditions that make freedom feel safe.

A home is not less a home because it has a foundation. A bridge is not less elegant because it has engineering beneath it. A body is not less alive because it depends on systems working in coordination. Love is not less human because it has architecture. It becomes more livable because it has architecture.

The resistance to structure often comes from the fear that intention will reduce feeling. But the opposite is often true. When the relationship has no structure, feeling has to carry too much. Every emotional shift becomes significant. Every misunderstanding feels larger. Every silence is interpreted. Every conflict threatens the bond because there is no reliable system underneath it. Feeling becomes overburdened. A structured relationship gives feeling a place to move without being asked to hold the entire relationship together.

It allows affection to be affection, not proof that everything is fine. It allows conflict to be conflict, not evidence that love is failing. It allows desire to change across seasons without immediately becoming panic. It allows feedback to enter without being treated as betrayal. It allows repair to be practiced without needing each rupture to redefine the whole relationship. Strategic love creates enough stability for the relationship to remain emotionally alive.

This is also why strategic love must include adaptation. A relationship cannot be designed once and then left untouched. No serious system works that way. Conditions change. People change. Stressors change. Bodies change. Families change. Work changes. Dreams change. Wounds surface. Capacities develop. Old agreements stop fitting. New needs emerge. A relationship that refuses to adapt becomes loyal to an earlier version of itself at the expense of the present one.

Many couples suffer not because they made the wrong commitments, but because they never revised the system after life changed.

They keep trying to communicate the way they communicated in a different season. They keep dividing responsibilities according to an old reality. They keep expecting desire, energy, patience, or availability to look the way it once did. They treat change as evidence that someone has failed, when often change is simply evidence that the system needs to be updated. Strategic love expects revision (Senge, 2006; Falconier et al., 2015).

It does not panic when the relationship needs to change shape. It asks what the current season requires. It asks what no longer works. It asks what has become too costly. It asks what needs more protection, more honesty, more attention, or more space. It does not interpret every need for adjustment as proof that the relationship is weak. It understands that living systems remain healthy by adapting.

Adaptation is not compromise in the shallow sense of each person giving up enough to keep the peace. Adaptation is the intelligent reorganization of the system so the relationship can continue to support the people inside it. Sometimes that means creating new agreements. Sometimes it means letting go of roles that once made sense. Sometimes it means acknowledging that one person has grown in a direction the relationship has not yet learned how to hold. Sometimes it means facing the truth that a pattern cannot continue without damaging the relationship further. Strategic love is willing to ask what the relationship must become in order to remain honest.

That willingness requires courage because not every answer will be comfortable. Some answers will require one person to become more accountable. Some will require both people to grieve the way things used to be. Some will reveal that affection remains but the system is no longer safe, mutual, or capable of growth. Strategy does not guarantee preservation. It guarantees clearer seeing.

This matters because intentional love is sometimes misunderstood as a way to save every relationship. It is not. Some relationships cannot become learning systems because one or both people refuse the work required. Some systems are too unsafe, too one-sided, too organized around control, denial, contempt, or avoidance. Some relationships contain real love but lack the accountability necessary to make love livable. Some patterns have done enough damage that the healthiest direction is not repair, but release. Strategic love does not mean staying at any cost. It means choosing with clarity rather than confusion.

Sometimes the most strategic act of love is to rebuild. Sometimes it is to renegotiate. Sometimes it is to set a boundary that the system can no longer ignore. Sometimes it is to stop participating in a cycle that has become destructive. Sometimes it is to leave with enough honesty to understand what happened and enough responsibility not to repeat the same architecture elsewhere.

A mature framework for love must include that possibility. Otherwise, strategy becomes just another form of romantic persistence, another way of making endurance sound noble even when endurance is no longer wise. But when both people are willing, strategic love can become one of the most generous forms of care.

It says, "I will not leave the health of this relationship to accident."

It says, "I will not assume love is strong simply because it exists."

It says, "I will pay attention to what we are becoming."

It says, "I will take responsibility for the patterns I bring, the meanings I assign, the repairs I owe, and the future I am helping create."

This kind of love is active without being anxious. It is intentional without being controlling. It is disciplined without being rigid. It understands that relationships are shaped not by occasional declarations but by repeated participation. The responsibility you now carry is the responsibility of awareness.

Once you understand that the system is being shaped, you cannot entirely return to the innocence of believing the outcome has nothing to do with repeated interaction. You may still feel confused. You may still react poorly. You may still fall into old patterns. Awareness does not make anyone perfect. But it does change what can honestly be ignored. You now know that patterns matter. You know that the problem is rarely just the problem. You know that what feels right at the beginning may not be enough to sustain what comes later. You know that personal mastery is not optional because the self you bring under stress becomes part of the system. You know that mental models shape what you believe is happening, even when the evidence is incomplete. You know that two people can love each other and still fail to become a team. You know that repair requires more than apology. You know that a relationship either learns or repeats.

That knowledge is not meant to burden you. It is meant to give you agency. But agency is not always comfortable because it removes the simplicity of helplessness. It becomes harder to say, "This is just how relationships go." It becomes harder to blame everything on timing, chemistry, personality, or fate. It becomes harder to pretend that avoiding the pattern is the same as changing it. Awareness gives you a choice. You can continue by default, or you can build with intention.

To build with intention, the relationship must become something both people are willing to look at directly. Not constantly. Not obsessively. But honestly. The relationship must be allowed to have a state of health that can be discussed. It must be allowed to drift and be brought back. It must be allowed to reveal weakness without immediately being condemned as failing. It must be allowed to need attention before crisis.

This may be one of the most practical definitions of strategic love: paying attention before the relationship makes neglect impossible to ignore.

A relationship that receives attention only when it is breaking will eventually learn to break in order to receive attention. A concern that matters only when it becomes a threat will escalate until it is taken seriously. A need that is heard only when it becomes resentment will learn resentment as a language. A partner who is believed only when they are ready to leave will begin to experience the relationship as responsive only to desperation. Strategic love responds earlier.

It treats small signals as worthy of care. It does not require pain to become severe before it becomes legitimate. It does not treat feedback as an inconvenience. It understands that early attention is not drama; it is maintenance of the living system. This is the kind of maintenance that does not diminish love. It protects it.

There is a difference between maintaining a relationship and merely preserving it. Preservation keeps something from ending. Maintenance keeps something capable of functioning. A preserved relationship may remain intact while becoming increasingly brittle. A maintained relationship receives the attention necessary to stay flexible, responsive, and alive. Strategic love is maintenance in the deeper sense.

It asks whether the relationship is still working, not only whether it still exists. It asks whether both people are still known, not only whether they are still together. It asks whether repair is real, not only whether conflict has ended. It asks whether the relationship is moving toward the life both people want, not simply whether it is avoiding collapse. That kind of attention requires rhythm.

A relationship cannot depend on rare, intense conversations to do all its developmental work. Those conversations may matter, but they are not enough. The system needs ordinary ways of staying in contact with itself. It needs moments where truth can enter before it hardens. It needs a culture where feedback is not saved for crisis. It needs a way for both people to say, "This is what I am noticing," without the sentence being treated as an attack.

The rhythm may be informal. It may emerge through conversation, shared reflection, quiet honesty at the end of a long week, or the willingness to pause when something feels off. The form matters less than the function. The relationship needs some recurring way to ask: Are we aligned? Are we avoiding anything? Are we repairing what we say we are repairing? Are we becoming more connected or simply more accustomed to the distance?

These questions are not meant to keep the relationship under examination at all times. They are meant to prevent the relationship from becoming a stranger to itself.

A relationship becomes a stranger to itself when the story people tell about it no longer matches the system they are living in. They say they are fine, but both are careful. They say they communicate, but the most important truths are avoided. They say they trust each other, but both are monitoring. They say they have moved on, but the same wound keeps appearing in new forms. They say the relationship is strong because it has lasted, but longevity has begun to stand in for vitality. Strategic love is willing to update the story.

It asks the relationship to be known as it is, not as it was imagined, not as it appeared in the beginning, and not as either person wants to present it to the world. This honesty can be uncomfortable because it may reveal gaps between image and reality. But a relationship cannot be strengthened by loyalty to an inaccurate story. It must be strengthened by contact with truth.

Truth does not have to be harsh. In fact, truth delivered without care often becomes another injury. But truth must be allowed to exist. A relationship that cannot tolerate truth cannot develop. It can only perform. Strategic love chooses development over performance.

This means it is less interested in appearing successful than in becoming healthy. It does not define strength by the absence of visible problems. It defines strength by the capacity to face problems without losing the humanity of the people involved. It understands that the strongest relationships are not always the ones that look effortless. They are often the ones that have learned how to work with difficulty without making difficulty the whole identity of the relationship. There is dignity in that kind of love.

It is not naive. It does not pretend that affection protects people from their patterns. It does not make chemistry responsible for compatibility. It does not treat time as proof of growth. It does not confuse staying with building. It is willing to look at the relationship as a living structure that must be cared for if it is going to endure with integrity. Integrity matters here.

A relationship has integrity when its structure matches its stated values. If the couple says they value honesty, then honesty must have a place to go. If they value respect, then respect must survive conflict. If they value growth, then feedback must be usable. If they value partnership, then stress cannot always be handled in isolation. If they value trust, then consistency must become visible enough for the system to rely on it. Integrity is not perfection. It is alignment between promise and pattern.

No relationship will maintain that alignment flawlessly. People will fail each other in small and sometimes significant ways. They will misunderstand, react, avoid, assume, and hurt. Strategic love does not demand a relationship without rupture. It asks whether rupture is followed by learning. It asks whether the system becomes more capable because of what it has been through. This is where love as a choice becomes more complex than the phrase usually suggests.

People often say love is a choice, but the statement can become too simple if it is not examined. Love is not only the choice to stay. It is not only the choice to keep caring when feeling is less intense. It is not only the choice to recommit after difficulty. Those choices matter, but they are incomplete. Love is also the choice to tell the truth. The choice to repair. The choice to listen when defensiveness would be easier. The choice to examine the mental model instead of obeying it. The choice to return after taking space. The choice to stop using old pain as permission for present harm. The choice to adapt when the old structure no longer works. The choice to stop preserving a relationship in a form that damages the people inside it.

Love as a choice is not a single decision. It is a pattern of decisions. It is made visible in the repeated moments where the relationship could become automatic and someone chooses awareness instead. This is why strategic love is not grand most of the time. It is ordinary (Hayes et al., 2012; Daks & Rogge, 2020).

It is found in the way a person enters a difficult conversation. In the way they handle the first sign of defensiveness. In the way they speak when they could punish. In the way they listen when they could prepare a counterargument. In the way they take responsibility without demanding immediate forgiveness. In the way they notice drift before resentment becomes easier than repair. It is found in the repeated decision to protect the future from the unconsciousness of the present.

That sentence may be one of the simplest ways to understand the work of this book. A relationship is always becoming something. Every interaction contributes to that becoming. Every avoided conversation, every honest repair, every repeated assumption, every moment of accountability, every pattern left alone, every act of courage, every withdrawal, every return—all of it enters the system. The future of the relationship is not built in the future. It is built in the patterns being reinforced now.

This is not meant to create fear. It is meant to create respect for the ordinary. Many people underestimate the ordinary because they are waiting for the defining moment. The betrayal. The proposal. The crisis. The decision. The breakthrough. The ending. But relationships are most often shaped before those moments arrive. They are shaped in daily repetitions that seem too small to carry consequence until consequence has accumulated. Strategic love honors the ordinary as the place where the relationship is actually made.

It does not wait for crisis to become conscious. It does not wait for distance to become obvious. It does not wait for a partner to stop trying before taking their feedback seriously. It does not wait for the system to fail before asking what it needs. It pays attention while there is still room to respond. This is the way forward.

Not a formula. Not a guarantee. Not a promise that every relationship can be repaired, strengthened, or made into what the people inside it hoped it would become. Love is too human for guarantees. Systems are influenced by willingness, safety, maturity, history, harm, capacity, and circumstance. There will always be limits. There will always be relationships where clarity arrives not to save the system, but to reveal that it cannot continue as it is. But even there, the framework matters.

A person who understands love as a system does not leave with only the story that love failed. They leave with knowledge. They understand what was built, what was missing, what was repeated, what was ignored, what they contributed, what they tolerated, what they could not change alone, and what they will need to build differently next time. That knowledge is not a consolation prize. It is the beginning of a different future.

For relationships that continue, the way forward is equally demanding and equally hopeful. It asks both people to become students of the relationship they are creating. To keep seeing the system. To keep practicing personal mastery. To keep questioning mental models. To keep moving from me to us. To keep defining what love is made of under the conditions they actually live in. To keep learning, repairing, adapting, and choosing direction over drift.

This is not work in the sense of drudgery. It is work in the sense that all meaningful creation is work. A business is built. A craft is developed. A body is trained. A home is cared for. A life is shaped. We do not think these things are less meaningful because they require attention. We understand that attention is part of what makes them possible. Love deserves the same respect.

The inherited story made love sound like something that should prove itself by requiring little. But a more mature story understands that effort is not evidence against love. Effort may be evidence that love has moved beyond fantasy into construction. The question is not whether love requires effort. The question is whether the effort is producing greater capacity, greater honesty, greater trust, and greater life inside the relationship. Effort without learning becomes exhaustion. Effort with direction becomes growth. Strategic love is effort with direction.

It is not frantic. It does not chase the relationship. It does not try to control every outcome. It does not turn love into constant analysis. It simply refuses to abandon the system to unconscious repetition. It asks what is being built and whether that structure can hold the people living inside it. That question should remain with the reader beyond this book. What are we building?

Not what do we feel in our best moments. Not what do we intend when everything is calm. Not what do we hope the relationship becomes if enough time passes. What are we building through what we repeat, avoid, repair, define, ignore, and choose?

The answer may be encouraging. It may reveal a relationship that is already learning, already adapting, already stronger than either person realized. It may reveal a system that has been strained but not broken, one that needs more structure, more honesty, more repair, but still has the willingness required to grow.

The answer may also be sobering. It may reveal that the relationship has relied too long on feeling, history, potential, or endurance. It may show that one person has been carrying the work of two. It may reveal that peace has been purchased through silence, that trust has been weakened by repeated patterns, or that the system is not yet safe enough for the kind of vulnerability being asked of it. Either way, the answer is useful. Clarity is useful.

This book began with the illusion of love because every new way of seeing has to begin by challenging the old one. The old illusion said that love would work if it was real enough, strong enough, right enough. It taught people to trust feeling as proof, connection as compatibility, chemistry as direction, and commitment as structure. It made love passive, even while making it emotionally powerful. The systems view offers something more demanding. It says love is real, but reality is not enough. Love must function.

It must have patterns that support it, feedback that informs it, repair that restores it, assumptions that can be questioned, and people inside it who are willing to learn. It must be built not only from emotion, but from repeated acts of consciousness. This does not make love smaller. It makes love more honest. And honesty, when joined with care, gives love a better chance of becoming durable.

The final movement of this book is not away from romance. It is away from passivity. Romance still matters. Tenderness still matters. Desire, beauty, delight, affection, and the inexplicable pull toward another person still matter. But they are not diminished by structure. They are protected by it. The candle still needs a room where the wind cannot extinguish it. The feeling still needs a system where it can survive contact with life. Love is not less meaningful because it has to be built. It is more meaningful because two people choose to build it with awareness.

The way forward, then, is not to abandon the mystery of love, but to stop hiding inside mystery when structure is required. It is not to explain every feeling, but to understand that feelings move through systems. It is not to make relationships perfect, but to make them more capable of truth, repair, adaptation, and shared life.

A strategic relationship does not ask, "How do we avoid ever struggling?"

It asks, "How do we become the kind of system that can meet struggle without losing ourselves or each other?"

It does not ask, "How do we keep the beginning alive forever?"

It asks, "How do we build something worthy of what the beginning made possible?"

It does not ask, "How do we prove this is love?"

It asks, "How do we help this love become livable, trustworthy, and wise?"

These are mature questions. They do not offer the emotional simplicity of the inherited story. They do not promise certainty. They do not guarantee that every relationship will last. But they make love workable in a way fantasy never could. They return responsibility to the people inside the relationship. And with responsibility comes possibility. The possibility of seeing the pattern before it becomes fate. The possibility of repairing before distance hardens. The possibility of speaking before silence becomes the architecture. The possibility of adapting before the system breaks under old assumptions. The possibility of building a relationship that is not merely endured, but consciously shaped. That is strategic love. Not cold love. Not managed love. Not love reduced to a plan. Love with enough awareness to protect what matters. Love with enough humility to learn. Love with enough discipline to become more than a feeling. Love with enough direction to move forward.

And perhaps this is the quiet truth at the center of it all: love does not become less real when we understand how it works. It becomes more available to us. More visible. More capable of being cared for. More capable of carrying the weight we so often place upon it without knowing what we are asking it to hold. The illusion taught us to wait for love to prove itself. The system teaches us to participate in what love becomes. That participation is the way forward. Not once. Not only when the relationship is in danger. Not only when the feeling is strong. But again and again, in the ordinary places where love is either strengthened or slowly surrendered. A relationship is not only something you find. It is something you build. And once you understand that, the question is no longer whether love will happen to you in the right way. The question is whether, when love arrives, you will know how to help it become something that can last.

EPILOGUE

What Love Becomes When It Can Learn

A relationship is not only remembered by how it begins. It is remembered by what it becomes.

The beginning matters. It carries energy, hope, attraction, recognition, and the emotional force that makes another person feel significant enough to disrupt the ordinary pattern of life. Without that beginning, most relationships would never move forward. There is dignity in the first feeling, in the moment when attention gathers around another person and something in the self becomes willing to open, risk, imagine, and move. But the beginning is not the whole truth of love. It is the doorway. What happens after the doorway is where the relationship is made.

This is the part most people were never fully taught to see. They were taught to recognize love by its emotional intensity, its ease, its sense of rightness, its promise of belonging. They were taught to look for the person, the feeling, the connection, the sign. They were taught, often without anyone saying it directly, that if love was real enough, it would know how to become what it needed to become. But love does not become durable simply because it is real. It becomes durable when it is understood, practiced, repaired, adapted, and consciously shaped.

That is the shift this book has been asking the reader to make. Not a shift away from love, but a shift into a more mature understanding of it. Love is not diminished when it is seen as a system. It is not made less intimate because it has patterns. It is not made less beautiful because it requires structure. To see love clearly is not to strip it of meaning. It is to give meaning somewhere to live.

The illusion of love asks feeling to carry the relationship. The system of love asks the relationship to become capable of carrying feeling. That difference changes everything.

When love is understood only as feeling, every change in feeling becomes alarming. Distance feels like loss. Conflict feels like evidence. Effort feels like failure. A difficult season feels like proof that something essential has disappeared. People begin to chase the beginning, trying to recover the version of the relationship that existed before stress, disappointment, routine, and difference made the system visible.

But when love is understood as a system, change becomes information. Not automatically good information, and not information to be ignored, but information that can be examined. A conflict may reveal an old pattern. A distance may reveal an unmet need. A recurring argument may reveal a feedback loop. A painful reaction may reveal a mental model that has been operating beneath awareness. A breakdown may reveal not the absence of love, but the absence of structure required to sustain it. This does not make love easier. It makes it more workable.

Workability matters because relationships are not sustained by insight alone. It is possible to understand the pattern and still repeat it. It is possible to name the wound and still protect oneself in the same way. It is possible to know that defensiveness blocks repair and still defend. It is possible to know that withdrawal creates distance and still disappear when overwhelmed. Human beings are not transformed merely because they can describe themselves accurately. Change requires practice.

This is where love becomes less passive and more responsible. A relationship changes when awareness becomes behavior. When the person who would have defended pauses long enough to listen. When the person who would have withdrawn names the need for space and returns. When the person who would have accused reveals the fear beneath the accusation. When the person who would have apologized quickly stays long enough to understand impact. When both people begin to treat the pattern as something they are creating together and therefore something they must learn to change together. This is not dramatic most of the time. It is ordinary.

The most important changes in a relationship often happen in moments no one else would notice. A softer beginning. A clearer request. A return after silence. A truth spoken before resentment hardens. A correction received without collapse. A boundary respected without punishment. An apology followed by different behavior. These moments may not look like transformation from the outside, but they are the places where the system learns. A relationship learns through repeated difference (Stokes & Baer, 1977; Baer et al., 1968).

Not through one perfect conversation. Not through one emotional breakthrough. Not through one weekend of reconnection. A system that has been built through repetition must be rebuilt through repetition. The new pattern has to appear often enough, under enough pressure, that the relationship begins to believe it. Trust begins to return not because someone insists they have changed, but because the system keeps encountering evidence of change. This is why love that can learn becomes stronger than love that merely hopes.

Hope is not unimportant. Hope can keep people engaged long enough to try again. It can soften despair. It can preserve the possibility of repair before the system has learned how to hold. But hope without evidence eventually becomes exhausting. Hope must be joined to action, pattern, accountability, and adaptation. Otherwise, it asks the future to do what the present refuses to build. A learning relationship does not live on hope alone. It produces evidence.

Evidence that difficult conversations can end differently. Evidence that feedback can be received. Evidence that the same injury does not have to repeat in the same form. Evidence that truth can enter without destroying the bond. Evidence that both people are willing to be changed by what the relationship has revealed. This willingness is the heart of mature love.

Not the willingness to lose oneself. Not the willingness to endure indefinitely. Not the willingness to accept what is unsafe, one-sided, or chronically unaccountable. Mature love is not measured by how much harm a person can absorb while calling it commitment. It is measured by the capacity to remain honest about what the relationship is becoming and to respond with integrity to what that honesty reveals. Sometimes that integrity leads to repair. Sometimes it leads to boundaries. Sometimes it leads to rebuilding. Sometimes it leads to an ending.

A systems view of love does not require every relationship to continue. It requires every relationship to be seen more truthfully. Some systems are capable of learning. Some are not. Some contain enough safety, humility, mutuality, and accountability to become stronger through examination. Others use the language of love to avoid responsibility, the language of repair to delay change, or the language of commitment to preserve a structure that continues to wound. Clarity matters in both cases (Watzlawick et al., 1967; Minuchin, 1974).

If a relationship can learn, clarity becomes the beginning of growth. If a relationship cannot learn, clarity becomes the beginning of release. Either way, the person who sees the system leaves the illusion behind. They no longer have to reduce the story to whether love was real or not real, whether they chose correctly or incorrectly, whether the feeling meant something or meant nothing. They can ask better questions. What did we build? What did we repeat? What did we avoid? What did we reinforce? What did we fail to repair? What did I bring into this system? What did the relationship reveal about the structure love requires?

These questions do not erase grief. They do not make disappointment painless. They do not turn loss into a lesson so quickly that the human cost disappears. But they do give pain a different kind of meaning. They prevent experience from becoming only injury. They allow a person to carry forward knowledge rather than only fear. That knowledge changes the next relationship.

It changes the way a person listens to feeling without surrendering judgment to it. It changes the way they evaluate connection without mistaking it for compatibility. It changes the way they notice early patterns, define values, observe their own reactions, and ask whether the relationship is becoming capable rather than merely compelling. It changes what they tolerate, what they question, what they build, and what they refuse to build again. This is one of the quiet forms of resilience. Not the resilience that simply survives what happened. The resilience that understands what happened well enough not to repeat it unconsciously.

Love, seen this way, becomes less about finding certainty and more about building capacity. The capacity to tell the truth. The capacity to stay present without losing oneself. The capacity to repair. The capacity to adapt. The capacity to revise old models when they distort the present. The capacity to move from individual protection into shared responsibility. The capacity to let the relationship become wiser than either person was at the beginning. That last capacity may be the most important (Senge, 2006; Daks & Rogge, 2020; Barraca et al., 2025).

A relationship that can learn becomes more than a container for two people's histories. It becomes a place where those histories are not simply reenacted. It becomes a system where old patterns can be noticed before they become destiny, where inherited assumptions can be questioned before they become rules, where pain can become information before it becomes identity. This is what love becomes when it can learn. Not perfect. Not effortless. Not untouched by fear, conflict, disappointment, or change. But conscious. Responsive. Capable. Alive.

A conscious relationship does not depend on the illusion that love should require no structure. It knows that structure is not the enemy of tenderness. It knows that attention is not the enemy of romance. It knows that feedback is not the enemy of safety. It knows that repair is not the enemy of commitment. It knows that strategy is not the enemy of feeling. It knows that what is cared for has a better chance of lasting.

This kind of love asks more of us than the inherited story did. It asks us to stop using intensity as proof, intention as defense, apology as performance, and endurance as the highest measure of devotion. It asks us to become more responsible for the systems we participate in creating. It asks us to notice what our patterns teach the people who love us. It asks us to understand that what we do repeatedly becomes the emotional climate someone else lives in. That is not a small responsibility. But neither is love.

To love another person is not only to feel something toward them. It is to participate in the conditions under which they experience closeness, trust, safety, truth, and belonging. It is to recognize that the relationship is not an abstract idea floating above behavior. It is built in the tone, the timing, the silence, the return, the repair, the question, the assumption interrupted before it becomes accusation, the courage to say what is true before truth becomes resentment. Love lives in the system. And the system lives in what is repeated.

This does not mean every moment must be controlled. A relationship that becomes overly managed can lose its breath. Love needs ease. It needs play, humor, sensuality, rest, surprise, quiet, and the unplanned grace of simply enjoying another person. The point of structure is not to make every moment productive. The point of structure is to protect the conditions in which ease can return without denial. Ease that depends on avoidance is fragile. Ease that rests on repair is different. It has been earned.

There is a kind of peace that comes only after the relationship has learned how to hold truth. It is not the peace of never being disturbed. It is the peace of knowing that disturbance does not have to become destruction. It is the peace of knowing that a difficult conversation can be survived, that feedback can be used, that distance can be named, that repair can be practiced, that the system has more than one way to respond. That peace is not passive. It is built.

The reader who has followed this argument from the beginning has been asked to give up a simpler story of love. That is not always easy. Simple stories are comforting because they ask less of perception. They let us believe that love is either right or wrong, present or absent, destined or doomed. They allow us to locate failure in the person, the timing, the choice, or the feeling. Sometimes those explanations contain truth. But they rarely contain enough truth to help us build differently.

The systems view is more demanding because it does not let us remain innocent in quite the same way. It asks us to see the pattern beneath the event, the model beneath the reaction, the reinforcement beneath the behavior, the structure beneath the feeling. It asks us to see love not only as something we experience, but as something we help create. That can feel heavy at first. Then, slowly, it becomes liberating.

Because if love is something we help create, then we are not only waiting to be chosen by the right feeling. We are not only hoping the relationship remains easy enough to survive. We are not only measuring the future by the intensity of the beginning. We are participating. We are observing. We are learning. We are building. And what is built consciously can be built more wisely.

There is no final arrival in this work. No relationship reaches a point where learning is complete. The system will continue to encounter new seasons, new pressures, new vulnerabilities, new forms of difference. The question is not whether change will come. It will. The question is whether the relationship has become capable of meeting change without losing its integrity. That is the work that continues after the last page. To notice drift before it becomes distance. To repair before pain becomes architecture. To question the story before it becomes certainty. To choose direction before reaction chooses for you. To keep asking what the relationship is becoming through what is being repeated. These are not tasks to complete once. They are practices of relational life.

Love that can learn is not a finished product. It is a living system. It remains alive because the people inside it remain willing to see, adjust, repair, and grow. It remains alive because it is not defended against truth. It remains alive because it has a structure strong enough to hold change and flexible enough not to mistake change for failure. This is what the illusion could never teach. The illusion taught that love should prove itself by feeling right. The learning relationship teaches that love proves itself by becoming more capable over time. Capable of truth. Capable of repair. Capable of adaptation. Capable of shared meaning. Capable of holding two human beings as they actually are, not only as they appeared in the beginning. That is what love becomes when it matures. Not less emotional. More responsible. Not less beautiful. More durable. Not less mysterious. More fully understood.

A relationship is not only something you find. It is something you shape, something you reinforce, something you repair, something you protect, something you learn how to build while it is also building you.

The question is not whether love will ever feel effortless again. Sometimes it will. There will be moments of ease, tenderness, laughter, desire, and quiet belonging that feel almost simple. But if the relationship has learned, those moments will no longer have to carry the burden of proving everything. They can simply be lived. The deeper question is whether love has become strong enough to survive the moments when it is not effortless. Whether it has a system. Whether it has awareness. Whether it has repair. Whether it has direction. Whether it can learn. If it can, then love becomes more than a feeling that once arrived with force. It becomes a relationship with a future. Not a guaranteed future. A built one.

BIBLIOGRAPHY

Ainsworth, M. D. S., Blehar, M. C., Waters, E., & Wall, S. (1978). Patterns of attachment: A psychological study of the strange situation. Lawrence Erlbaum Associates.

Argyris, C., & Schön, D. A. (1978). Organizational learning: A theory of action perspective. Addison-Wesley.

Baer, D. M., Wolf, M. M., & Risley, T. R. (1968). Some current dimensions of applied behavior analysis. Journal of Applied Behavior Analysis, 1(1), 91–97. https://doi.org/10.1901/jaba.1968.1-91

Bandura, A. (1977). Self-efficacy: Toward a unifying theory of behavioral change. Psychological Review, 84(2), 191–215. https://doi.org/10.1037/0033-295X.84.2.191

Barraca, J., Polanski, T., Duarte-Díaz, A., & Perestelo-Pérez, L. (2025). Acceptance and commitment therapy for couples: A systematic review and meta-analysis. Journal of Contextual Behavioral Science, 35, 100867. https://doi.org/10.1016/j.jcbs.2024.100867

Baucom, K. J. W., Sevier, M., Eldridge, K. A., Doss, B. D., & Christensen, A. (2011). Observed communication in couples two years after integrative and traditional behavioral couple therapy: Outcome and link with five-year follow-up. Journal of Consulting and Clinical Psychology, 79(5), 565–576. https://doi.org/10.1037/a0025121

Beasley, C. C., & Ager, R. (2019). Emotionally focused couples therapy: A systematic review of its effectiveness over the past 19 years. Journal of Evidence-Based Social Work, 16(2), 144–159. https://doi.org/10.1080/23761407.2018.1563013

Beck, A. T. (1976). Cognitive therapy and the emotional disorders. International Universities Press.

Beck, A. T., Rush, A. J., Shaw, B. F., & Emery, G. (1979). Cognitive therapy of depression. Guilford Press.

Blanchard, V. L., Hawkins, A. J., Baldwin, S. A., & Fawcett, E. B. (2009). Investigating the effects of marriage and relationship education on couples' communication skills: A meta-analytic study. Journal of Family Psychology, 23(2), 203–214. https://doi.org/10.1037/a0015211

Bloch, L., Haase, C. M., & Levenson, R. W. (2014). Emotion regulation predicts marital satisfaction: More than a wives' tale. Emotion, 14(1), 130–144.https://doi.org/10.1037/a0034272

Bowen, M. (1978). Family therapy in clinical practice. Jason Aronson.

Bowlby, J. (1969). Attachment and loss: Vol. 1. Attachment. Basic Books.

Bradbury, T. N., & Fincham, F. D. (1990). Attributions in marriage: Review and critique. Psychological Bulletin, 107(1), 3–33. https://doi.org/10.1037/0033-2909.107.1.3

Candel, O. S., & Turliuc, M. N. (2019). Insecure attachment and relationship satisfaction: A meta-analysis of actor and partner associations. Personality and Individual Differences, 147, 190–199. https://doi.org/10.1016/j.paid.2019.04.037

Christensen, A., Atkins, D. C., Baucom, B., & Yi, J. (2010). Marital status and satisfaction five years following a randomized clinical trial comparing traditional versus integrative behavioral couple therapy. Journal of Consulting and Clinical Psychology, 78(2), 225–235. https://doi.org/10.1037/a0018132

Daks, J. S., & Rogge, R. D. (2020). Examining the correlates of psychological flexibility in romantic relationship and family dynamics: A meta-analysis. Journal of Contextual Behavioral Science, 18, 214–238. https://doi.org/10.1016/j.jcbs.2020.09.010

Edmondson, A. C. (1999). Psychological safety and learning behavior in work teams. Administrative Science Quarterly, 44(2), 350–383. https://doi.org/10.2307/2666999

Falconier, M. K., Jackson, J. B., Hilpert, P., & Bodenmann, G. (2015). Dyadic coping and relationship satisfaction: A meta-analysis. Clinical Psychology Review, 42, 28–46. https://doi.org/10.1016/j.cpr.2015.07.002

Forrester, J. W. (1968). Principles of systems. Wright-Allen Press.

Gottman, J. M. (1994). What predicts divorce? The relationship between marital processes and marital outcomes. Lawrence Erlbaum Associates.

Gottman, J. M., & Levenson, R. W. (1992). Marital processes predictive of later dissolution: Behavior, physiology, and health. Journal of Personality and Social Psychology, 63(2), 221–233. https://doi.org/10.1037/0022-3514.63.2.221

Gottman, J. M., & Silver, N. (2015). The seven principles for making marriage work: A practical guide from the country's foremost relationship expert (Rev. ed.). Harmony Books.

Greenberg, L. S., & Johnson, S. M. (1988). Emotionally focused therapy for couples. Guilford Press.

Gross, J. J. (1998). The emerging field of emotion regulation: An integrative review. Review of General Psychology, 2(3), 271–299. https://doi.org/10.1037/1089-2680.2.3.271

Gross, J. J., & John, O. P. (2003). Individual differences in two emotion regulation processes: Implications for affect, relationships, and well-being. Journal of Personality and Social Psychology, 85(2), 348–362. https://doi.org/10.1037/0022-3514.85.2.348

Hawkins, A. J., Blanchard, V. L., Baldwin, S. A., & Fawcett, E. B. (2008). Does marriage and relationship education work? A meta-analytic study. Journal of Consulting and Clinical Psychology, 76(5), 723–734. https://doi.org/10.1037/a0012584

Hayes, S. C., Luoma, J. B., Bond, F. W., Masuda, A., & Lillis, J. (2006). Acceptance and commitment therapy: Model, processes and outcomes. Behaviour Research and Therapy, 44(1), 1–25. https://doi.org/10.1016/j.brat.2005.06.006

Hayes, S. C., Strosahl, K. D., & Wilson, K. G. (2012). Acceptance and commitment therapy: The process and practice of mindful change (2nd ed.). Guilford Press.

Hazan, C., & Shaver, P. R. (1987). Romantic love conceptualized as an attachment process. Journal of Personality and Social Psychology, 52(3), 511–524. https://doi.org/10.1037/0022-3514.52.3.511

Jacobson, N. S., Christensen, A., Prince, S. E., Cordova, J., & Eldridge, K. (2000). Integrative behavioral couple therapy: An acceptance-based, promising new treatment for couple discord. Journal of Consulting and Clinical Psychology, 68(2), 351–355. https://doi.org/10.1037/0022-006X.68.2.351

Johnson, S. M. (2019). Attachment theory in practice: Emotionally focused therapy (EFT) with individuals, couples, and families. Guilford Press.

Johnson, S. M. (2020). The practice of emotionally focused couple therapy: Creating connection (3rd ed.). Routledge.

Kahneman, D. (2011). Thinking, fast and slow. Farrar, Straus and Giroux.

Kazdin, A. E. (1977). Assessing the clinical or applied importance of behavior change through social validation. Behavior Modification, 1(4), 427–452. https://doi.org/10.1177/014544557714001

Lazarus, R. S., & Folkman, S. (1984). Stress, appraisal, and coping. Springer Publishing Company.

Meadows, D. H. (2008). Thinking in systems: A primer (D. Wright, Ed.). Chelsea Green Publishing.

Minuchin, S. (1974). Families and family therapy. Harvard University Press.

Papp, L. M., Kouros, C. D., & Cummings, E. M. (2009). Demand-withdraw patterns in marital conflict in the home. Personal Relationships, 16(2), 285–300. https://doi.org/10.1111/j.1475-6811.2009.01223.x

Randall, A. K., & Bodenmann, G. (2009). The role of stress on close relationships and marital satisfaction. Clinical Psychology Review, 29(2), 105–115. https://doi.org/10.1016/j.cpr.2008.10.004

Ryan, R. M., & Deci, E. L. (2000). Self-determination theory and the facilitation of intrinsic motivation, social development, and well-being. American Psychologist, 55(1), 68–78. https://doi.org/10.1037/0003-066X.55.1.68

Schrodt, P., Witt, P. L., & Shimkowski, J. R. (2014). A meta-analytical review of the demand/withdraw pattern of interaction and its associations with individual, relational, and communicative outcomes. Communication Monographs, 81(1), 28–58. https://doi.org/10.1080/03637751.2013.813632

Senge, P. M. (2006). The fifth discipline: The art & practice of the learning organization (Rev. & updated ed.). Doubleday.

Skinner, B. F. (1953). Science and human behavior. Macmillan.

Smith, P. (2026). Exploring Marital Resilience Through the Lived Experiences and Perception of Spousal Support During Events of Shared Stressors (Order No. 32669734). Available from Dissertations & Theses @ Walden University; ProQuest One Academic. (3333479217). https://www.proquest.com/dissertations-theses/exploring-marital-resilience-through-lived/docview/3333479217/se-2

Sternberg, R. J. (1986). A triangular theory of love. Psychological Review, 93(2), 119–135. https://doi.org/10.1037/0033-295X.93.2.119

Stokes, T. F., & Baer, D. M. (1977). An implicit technology of generalization. Journal of Applied Behavior Analysis, 10(2), 349–367. https://doi.org/10.1901/jaba.1977.10-349

Tversky, A., & Kahneman, D. (1974). Judgment under uncertainty: Heuristics and biases. Science, 185(4157), 1124–1131. https://doi.org/10.1126/science.185.4157.1124

von Bertalanffy, L. (1968). General system theory: Foundations, development, applications. George Braziller.

Watzlawick, P., Beavin, J. H., & Jackson, D. D. (1967). Pragmatics of human communication: A study of interactional patterns, pathologies, and paradoxes. W. W. Norton & Company.

Wiebe, S. A., & Johnson, S. M. (2016). A review of the research in emotionally focused therapy for couples. Family Process, 55(3), 390–407. https://doi.org/10.1111/famp.12229

Wolf, M. M. (1978). Social validity: The case for subjective measurement or how applied behavior analysis is finding its heart. Journal of Applied Behavior Analysis, 11(2), 203–214. https://doi.org/10.1901/jaba.1978.11-203

ABOUT THE AUTHOR

Dr. Prince-James Smith is a cognitive psychologist, researcher, business strategist, entrepreneur, and human resources professional whose work bridges the gap between psychological theory and real-world transformation. With a Ph.D. in Cognitive Psychology, a Master of Science in Psychology, a Master of Philosophy in Psychology, and a Bachelor of Science in Business Administration and Change Management, Dr. Smith brings a unique blend of academic expertise, business insight, and practical leadership experience to every area of work.

For more than thirteen years, Dr. Smith has worked in business analytics, using data, patterns, and behavioral insights to help organizations make informed decisions and create meaningful change. As an entrepreneur for over a decade, Dr. Smith has developed businesses from the ground up, gaining firsthand experience in leadership, innovation, strategy, resilience, and the realities of building something with purpose and vision. In addition, with more than ten years of experience as a human resources manager, Dr. Smith has worked closely with individuals, teams, and organizations to support growth, improve communication, and strengthen workplace effectiveness.

Dr. Smith's academic research has long centered on relationships, communication, and resilience. The master's thesis focused on improving couple communication techniques, while the doctoral dissertation explored marital resilience. These areas of study reflect a deep commitment to understanding how people think, connect, adapt, and overcome challenges in both personal and professional settings.

Most importantly, Dr. Smith's education and professional experience are grounded in the belief that psychology should not remain only in textbooks or research journals. Instead, psychological and behavioral principles can be applied to practical, real-world solutions. Through this work, Dr. Smith helps individuals shift their perceptions, challenge limiting patterns, and embrace new ways of thinking that lead to personal growth, healthier relationships, stronger leadership, and lasting change.

This book reflects Dr. Smith's passion for combining knowledge, experience, and purpose to empower others to see themselves, their relationships, and their possibilities in a new light.

www.ingramcontent.com/pod-product-compliance
Lightning Source LLC
LaVergne TN
LVHW022216200926
848481LV00006B/1993
9798996226221